This Book belongs to Sally

WHSMITH
Complete
Freezer
Book

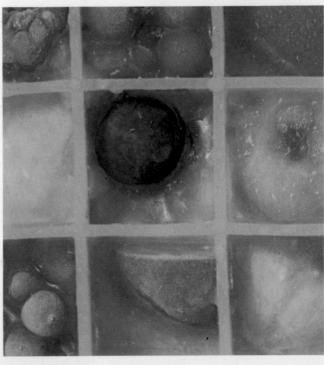

WHSMITH
Complete Freezer Book

Mary Norwak

this edition produced exclusively for

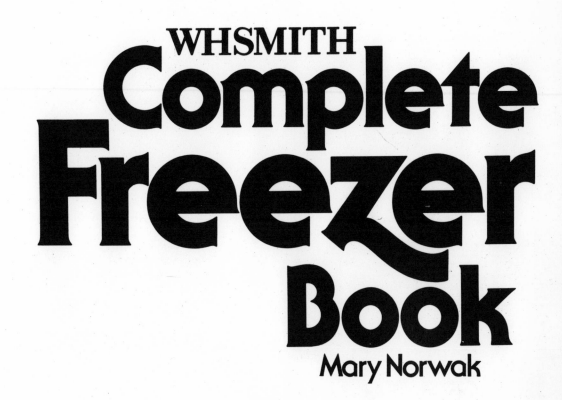 WHSMITH

Illustrations © Ward Lock and Orbis-Verlag für Publizistik 1978

Produced specially for W H Smith & Sons by Ward Lock Ltd,
116 Baker Street, London W1M 2BB, a member of the Pentos Group.

Designed by Mel Saunders

Text filmset in 12pt. 'Monophoto' Apollo
by Servis Filmsetting Limited, Manchester

Printed and bound in Singapore by
Toppan Printing Co.

ISBN 0 7063 4176 7

The Publisher and Author wish to thank the follow-
ing firms who have supplied photographs and
information for this book: Alcan Polyfoil Ltd;
Bacofoil Ltd; Bejam Freezer Food Centres Ltd;
Electrolux Ltd; Frigidaire Europe (General Motors
Ltd); Hoover Ltd and Philips Electrical Ltd.

Contents

Weights and Measures 6

Part I
Introduction 8
Your Freezer 10
Packing and Labelling 14
Bulk Buying and Cooking 19
Freezing Vegetables and Herbs 26
Freezing Fruit 35
Freezing Meat 47
Freezing Bacon 53
Freezing Poultry and Game 55
Freezing Fish and Shellfish 60
Freezing Dairy Produce 65
Freezing Bread, Cakes, Pastry and
    Sandwiches 69
Freezing Cooked Dishes 80
High Quality Storage Life 86

Part II
Soups 91
Pâtés 100
Fish Dishes 103
Poultry 113
Meat Dishes 118
Savoury Dishes, Pastries and Pasta 130
Vegetable Dishes 140
Sauces and Stuffings 154
Puddings 158
Breads, Cakes and Pastries 170
Index 190

Weights and Measures

WEIGHT

1 oz	= 25 grams
4 oz	= 100 grams
8 oz	= 225 grams
1 lb	= 450 grams
	(0·45 kg)

LIQUID CAPACITY

1 fl oz	= 25 ml
$\frac{1}{4}$ pt	= 125 ml
$\frac{1}{2}$ pt	= 250 ml
1 pt	= 500 ml
1 quart	= 1·13 litres

SPOONS

1 teaspoon	= 5 ml spoon
1 dessertspoon	= 10 ml spoon
1 tablespoon	= 15 ml spoon

SUGAR BOILING TEMPERATURES

Soft ball	237°F	114°C
Hard ball	247°F	119°C
Soft crack	280°F	140°C
Hard crack	310°F	154°C
Caramel	340°F	171°C

DOMESTIC OVEN TEMPERATURES

	ELECTRIC °F	CELSIUS °C	GAS
Very cool	225	110	$\frac{1}{4}$
Very cool	250	130	$\frac{1}{2}$
Very cool	275	140	1
Cool	300	150	2
Warm	325	170	3
Moderate	350	180	4
Fairly hot	375	190	5
Fairly hot	400	200	6
Hot	425	220	7
Very hot	450	230	8
Very hot	475	240	9

DEEP FAT FRYING TEMPERATURES

FOOD	BREAD BROWNS IN	FAT TEMPERATURE	OIL TEMPERATURE
Raw starchy foods doughnuts, fritters, chips (1st frying)	1$\frac{1}{4}$ minutes	325°–340°F 170°C	340°F 170°C
Fish in batter	1$\frac{1}{4}$ minutes	325°–340°F 170°C	340°F 170°C
Fish in egg and crumbs	1 minute	360°F 185°C	360°F 185°C
Scotch eggs	1 minute	350°F 180°C	350°F 180°C
Reheated foods potato straws, chips (2nd frying)	40 seconds	380°F 190°C	390°F 195°C

Complete Freezer Book
Part 1

Introduction

Freezing is a quick method of preserving fresh and cooked food safely. The activities of micro-organisms are slowed down as food approaches freezing point, and they become dormant at 0°F (−18°C). Home freezers with four-star marking are designed to bring the food down to this temperature, and to maintain it for storage. Most modern freezers have a fast-freeze compartment in which the temperature can be further reduced for short periods so that fresh food can be frozen quickly.

The advantages of home freezing, bulk buying and batch cooking are now appreciated by more and more people, both

town and country dwellers. An efficient home-freezing system can save money through economic purchasing of seasonal or commercially frozen raw materials, and can also save shopping and cooking time. Many women now work outside the home, and there is tremendous growth in the field of leisure activities and adult education, so that many families rarely eat together in the traditional way. A freezer in the home can simplify the problem of trying to shop at odd hours, can make it worthwhile to batch-cook at weekends, and can enable different members of a family to heat and eat dishes at their convenience, rather than relying on unhealthy snacks or expensive grills.

The well-run freezer can serve a dual purpose, combining the long-term storage of bulk raw materials from garden, farm or market, and commercially frozen foods, with the short-term storage of cooked dishes and leftovers which are meant to be used up quickly. A refrigerator is an essential partner to the freezer, for chilling food to be frozen, and for thawing food slowly but safely.

Your Freezer

Adaptable Freezing

Long-term storage is effective for the foods which you may buy cheaply from bulk suppliers; for farm and garden produce, and gluts of fresh food which are in season; also for special items, such as tropical fruits or rich cream, which you may get when on holiday, or which kind friends send you.

Short-term storage is a wonderful money-saver and way of varying meals by using cooked foods or leftovers. It is also useful if you do batch cookery of basic items such as simple sauces, for items such as bread which you need regularly, and for complete meals for sudden entertaining or emergency use.

Freezing is an easy process if you follow the basic instructions. These are not rigid rules but guide lines, showing how food can be kept well and retain flavour, colour and nutritive value. This book is designed for quick reference when preserving both raw materials and cooked foods. Types of food suitable for freezing are defined; but your individual requirements can only be assessed by experience, and by testing your favourite recipes under freezing conditions. The basic recipes included here are those which have proved successful in freezer storage and in subsequent cooking and eating.

The refrigerator is an invaluable aid to successful freezing. The freezer will function better if food is chilled in the refrigerator before being placed in the cabinet for freezing. The ice-making compartment of your refrigerator can also supply reserves of ice for rapidly chilling blanched vegetables and cooked dishes. Again, you can store large quantities of food temporarily in the refrigerator while the smaller recommended quantities are being frozen.

The refrigerator ice-making compartment can also be used for short-term storage of ice cream and other frozen products (see 'The Star System'). Frozen food should never be thawed quickly as rapid deterioration sets in, so the refrigerator is recommended for thawing almost all the items you freeze. The housewife who can assess her daily needs can transfer items from freezer to refrigerator storage first thing in the morning ready for later serving and further cooking if necessary.

The Star System

Frozen-food compartments on most British refrigerators are marked with stars in accordance with British Standards Specification No. 3739. This indicates recommended storage times for individual packets of commercially frozen foods.

* (one star) $-6°C$ or $21°F$ stores bought frozen food for one week, and ice cream for one day.
** (two star) $-12°C$ or $10°F$ stores bought frozen food for one month, and ice cream for two weeks.
*** (three star) $-18°C$ or $0°F$ stores bought frozen food for three months, and ice cream for one month.

Three-star frozen-food compartments are normally capable of freezing down to $0°F$ within 24 hours small quantities of fresh or cooked food, according to individual refrigerator manufacturers' instructions.

A true food freezer, however, is capable of always operating at $0°F$ ($-18°C$) and is additionally capable of freezing unfrozen food to this temperature without any significant change in the temperature of the food already being stored. It can also store food for many months or even a year rather than weeks.

Four Star Marking

This symbol, consisting of a rectangular frame

containing a large six-pointed star, and three small six-pointed stars in a curved frame distinguishes a true freezer compartment from the type above. The large star symbolises the food freezing capacity, and the three smaller stars (as used on frozen food storage compartments) indicate that most commercially-frozen foods can be stored up to three months. Manufacturers using this symbol must indicate in their instructions the maximum weight of food which can be frozen in 24 hours.

Insurance of Contents
The contents of a freezer can be valuable, particularly if large quantities of meat or game are stored. Only a small premium is usually required.

Running Costs

The cost of running a freezer will be affected by the size of the freezer cabinet and its design, as well as by the warmth of the room in which it stands. The number of times the cabinet is opened daily, and the length of time it is kept open will affect running costs, as will the amount of fresh food being frozen and the temperature at which it is put into the freezer. A well-packed freezer is more economical to run as the packages provide insulation, and current is wasted if it is being used to chill air in empty spaces. An upright freezer uses fractionally more current than a chest model as cold air 'escapes' more readily from an open door than from a lid.

Under average conditions, with the cabinet three-quarters full, each litre of food freezer space will use approximately ·06 of a unit each week in an ambient temperature of 18°C (there are 28·3 litres to each cubic foot). Smaller freezers below 283 litres (10 cu. ft) capacity tend to use slightly more than the ·06 unit average. As an example, a 56·5 litre (2 cu. ft) cabinet will use 4 units weekly; 113 litre (4 cu. ft) will use 8 units weekly; 141·5 litre (5 cu. ft) will use 10 units weekly.

Choosing a Freezer

The choice of a freezer will depend not only on the size of your family and the amount of your home produce but on the space available in kitchen or outhouse. Ideally, the freezer should be within easy reach of the cook, but excessive kitchen heat will put a heavy load on the cooling mechanism. Air must circulate freely round the freezer so that heat can be efficiently removed from the condenser.

The capacity of this large chest freezer will enable its owner to take full advantage of the economies of bulk buying.

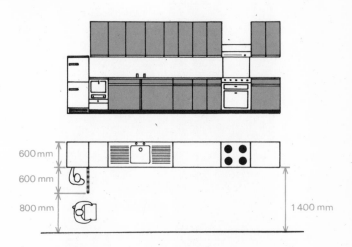

Site the freezer clear of the wall, well away from a cooker or fire.

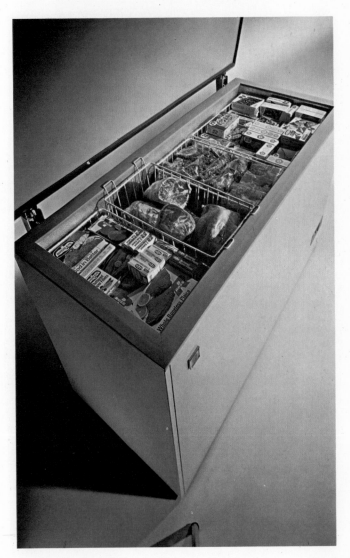

An easily accessible vertical fridge/freezer with a high storage capacity. The design is ideal for those with only a small kitchen area.

BELOW: *This vertical fridge/freezer shows just how much food can be stored in a relatively small unit for both short and long-term freezing.*

Dampness will damage both cabinet and motor.

Chest freezers are particularly suitable for locating in a garage or outhouse, and are excellent for bulk storage of such items as meat. Storage baskets make for tidiness and help to divide food to be used soon from that which is kept for long-term storage. Very large commercial sizes are usually designed as chests, and can represent considerable economy in purchasing. It is important that a chest freezer has a magnetic lid seal and a self-balancing lid.

Upright freezers are very convenient for packing, with separate shelves for different types of food. There may be some slight intermittent rise in temperature in upright freezers as doors are often left open. Upright freezers have their weight concentrated in a small area, and it is important to check that the floor will take the weight of the freezer chosen.

Combination refrigerator freezers are very useful when space is limited as in a town house or flat.

Special features to look for

Most freezers have a light which comes on when the electricity supply is connected and switched on; failure of the light means the power supply has been cut off and immediate investigation is necessary. Some freezers have a signal light connected to the thermostat which stays on as long as the cabinet temperature does not rise above a few degrees from the normal operating temperature.

Fast freezing compartments, switches and indicator lights are useful adjuncts to a freezer. Some freezers have a compartment divided by a panel or grid to keep still-unfrozen foods separate from stored foods while they are being processed. Some upright freezers have a shelf for fast freezing which is very useful for processing vegetables, cakes and pies which can be frozen before wrapping. The fast freezing switch cuts out thermostatic control so that the motor runs continuously; heat is thus removed from unfrozen food as quickly as possible and the stored foods do not rise in temperature. The switch must be returned to normal running as soon as possible; sometimes the switch is wired in conjunction with an indicator light to show when the motor is running continuously.

Other useful additions to a freezer are storage baskets, which aid tidiness. Locks are useful to avoid pilfering if the freezer is stored in an outhouse; they also prevent children opening the freezer and leaving it open.

Installing the Freezer
A newly installed freezer should be washed inside with warm water and dried thoroughly, then set at the recommended temperature for everyday use. The cabinet should be chilled for 12 hours before use.

Cleaning and Defrosting
Defrosting is normally carried out when ice is $\frac{1}{4}$ in/ 6 mm thick. Manufacturers' instructions should be followed for occasional defrosting, but build-ups of ice may be removed with a plastic scraper. Sharp tools or wire brushes should not be used. For complete defrosting, food should be removed to a refrigerator or wrapped in layers of newspapers and blankets in a cold place. After defrosting, the freezer should be wiped completely dry and run at the coldest setting for 30 minutes before replacing food. The machine should then continue to run at the coldest setting for a further $2\frac{1}{2}$ hours before the switch is returned to normal setting.

The inside of the freezer is best cleaned with a solution of 2 pints/1 litre water and 1 tablespoon bicarbonate of soda; the water should be lukewarm. Soap, detergent or caustic cleaners must not be used. The outside of the cabinet may be cleaned with warm soapy water and polished with enamel surface polish.

Power Failure
When power fails, the freezer is best checked first for local causes. The switch may have been turned off by mistake, or the fuse in the plug may have 'blown'.

The cabinet should be left shut when power has failed, so that the cold temperature is retained. Properly packed food will last about 12 hours safely, although this depends on the load of food and on insulation. A fully packed freezer will maintain a low temperature for a longer period.

Packing and Labelling

Freezing is not only an easy way of preserving both raw and cooked food, but it is also completely safe if the rules of hygiene are observed and food is correctly packed.

Good food will keep its quality and nutritive value in the freezer, but freezing cannot improve poor quality food.

Basic Freezing Procedure
1 All food for freezing must be processed quickly, according to the instructions.
2 Food must be thoroughly chilled before being put in the freezer to avoid raising the temperature of food already stored.
3 Food must be carefully packed to exclude air, and should be labelled for identification. A simple record of the food in the freezer will aid meal planning and encourage you to maintain a steady turnover.
4 Food should be frozen quickly, preferably against the cold surfaces of the cabinet, and at the recommended low temperature.
5 Frozen cooked food must never be thawed and then refrozen. Raw materials should not be thawed and refrozen, but may be made into cooked dishes and frozen.

Portions
Food should be prepared and packed in usable portions. Most people find it wise to prepare some large or family-sized packs and also a number of individual packs for use for single meals. Large packs of fruit and vegetables can be re-fastened after portions have been removed. A single portion of food will vary according to whether it is for a small child, a woman or a manual worker. Two people together usually eat slightly less than two single people.

Packaging Materials
All packaging should be moisture and vapour proof, waterproof and greaseproof; durable and resistant to low temperatures; easily handled, economically stored and free from smell. Suitable materials are indicated for various groups of foods; individual packing methods are described where necessary.

Waxed tubs Waxed tubs are available with flush airtight lids and with screw-on tops. Waxed cartons are also made with fitted lids in square and rectangular shapes, and there are tall containers with tuck-in lids, and special ones with polythene liners which are suitable for food subject to leakage.

Rigid plastic containers Most branded plastic boxes are suitable for freezer storage. Those with flexible sides can be slightly pressed to aid removal of contents.

Glass jars Screwtop preserving jars, bottles and honey jars may be used for freezing if tested for resistance to low temperature. Place an empty jar in a plastic bag in the freezer overnight; if it breaks, the bag will hold the pieces. Jars with 'shoulders' should not be used as this necessitates long thawing before the food can be turned out and used.

Polythene Polythene bags are useful for almost all freezer food, and are available in a wide variety of sizes; they should be of the special heavy quality designed for low temperatures. Polythene sheeting is easy to handle for wrapping meat, poultry and pies, and its transparency makes quick identification easy.

Foil and freezer paper Foil dishes are useful for dishes which are cooked before freezing and are later reheated, as one container may be used for all the processes. Heavy-duty foil sheeting is useful for overwrapping these dishes, and for packing both raw and cooked foods; it should be used with the dull side towards the food. Freezer paper is strong wrapping which is highly resistant to fat and grease, does not puncture easily, and has an uncoated outer surface on which labelling details may be written.

Microwave/freezer containers are the newest packs for the freezer. Foil containers cannot be used

Foil and polythene are ideal freezer wrappings and coloured labels aid identification.

for heating in a microwave, but the oven is invaluable for reheating frozen dishes. Therefore freezer packaging has been made in a material which is suitable for use in a microwave oven. The containers which include cake dishes, deep trays and loaf dishes can be used for microwave cooking dishes which can then be frozen in the same containers, which are again used for reheating. Alternatively, food may be cooked by conventional methods, then packaged in a microwave/freezer container in which it will be both frozen and reheated in the microwave oven.

All types of container and sheet wrapping must be firmly sealed. Bags can be closed with fasteners or heat-sealed with a special welding unit, or with a domestic iron used over thick paper. Special freezing tape with gum which is resistant to low temperatures must be used for finishing sheet-wrapped packages and sealing containers with lids.

Headspace and Air Exclusion

Containers with lids should be packed so that head-space from $\frac{1}{2}$–1 in/1·25–2·5 cm is left above the surface of the food to allow for expansion of contents, according to individual foods.

All sheet wrappings or bags must have the air pressed out so that the wrapping adheres closely to the food. When forming a parcel, the air can be pressed out with the hands. Air is most easily removed from bags by the insertion of a drinking straw at the closing, and by sucking the air out just before sealing.

Packaging

To avoid loss of quality, food should be carefully processed, packed, and then thawed or cooked quickly when needed. An enzyme is a type of protein which accelerates the chemical reactions in food. These reactions are slowed down by the freezing process, but thawing speeds up enzymic reaction. It therefore encourages rapid deterioration so that food is best thawed in a cold atmosphere such as a refrigerator, and must be eaten or cooked immediately after thawing.

Bad packaging causes a number of problems which will not render the food dangerous to eat, but which may cause an unattractive appearance, toughness and dryness, lack of flavour, or unpleasant mingling of flavours from different foods. Some of these are:

Dehydration and freezer burn Long storage and poor wrapping may result in the removal of moisture and juices, particularly from meat. This sometimes causes greyish-brown areas on food known as 'freezer burn'.

Oxidation and rancidity Oxygen from the air which penetrates wrappings reacts with fat cells in food to form chemicals which give meat and fish a bad taste and smell. Fried foods, fat meat and fish can suffer from this problem in the freezer. Salt accelerates this rancidity.

Broken packages and cross-flavourings Rough handling, sharp edges, brittle wrappings or over-filled containers may cause cracks or breakages which will result in dehydration or oxidation. This can also result in cross-flavouring with strongly flavoured foods, which may also spread smells and flavours if packages are not very strong or over-wrapped.

Flabbiness Limp and flabby fruit and vegetables are caused by slow freezing, and sometimes by the choice of varieties unsuitable for freezing, which must be subject to trial and error. Suitable varieties are recommended by seedsmen.

Ice crystals If too large a headspace is left on liquid foods in containers, a layer of ice crystals may form which will affect storage and flavour. Liquids can be shaken or stirred back into emulsion when heated or thawed. If the problem occurs in meat, fish, vegetables or fruit, it is usually because the

food has been slow-frozen so that moisture in the cells has expanded and frozen and broken surrounding tissues. This results in juices and flavour being lost.

Suitable Packing Materials
The most commonly used packaging materials for various types of food are indicated thus ◯.

Packaging Hints

Preliminary Wrapping
It is important to attend to any preliminary wrapping of food so that items can be easily separated for thawing. Sliced meat should be layered with sheets of cling-film or freezer tissue to separate the slices; bones or protuberances on meat or poultry should be covered with a padding of paper or foil; cakes without icing should be layered with separating paper.

Overwrapping
When packages are subject to heavy handling and possible puncture, or when there is danger of cross-flavouring, they should be overwrapped with ordinary brown paper, an extra layer of foil or polythene, or with stockinette (mutton cloth). An inside wrapping of stockinette on meat and poultry helps prevent freezer burn during long storage.

Sheet Wrapping
The food to be wrapped should be in the centre of the sheet of packaging material. Draw two sides of

FOOD	WAXED OR RIGID PLASTIC CONTAINERS	FOIL CONTAINERS	FOIL SHEETING	POLYTHENE BAGS OR SHEETING
Fresh Meat			◯	◯
Fresh Poultry and Game			◯	◯
Fresh Fish			◯	◯
Cooked Meat and Fish Dishes	◯	◯	◯	◯
Fresh Vegetables	◯			◯
Fresh Fruit (unsweetened or dry sugar pack)	◯			◯
Fresh Fruit (syrup pack)	◯			
Butter, Margarine and Fats		◯	◯	◯
Cheese			◯	◯
Milk and Cream	◯			
Eggs	◯	◯		
Soups and Sauces	◯	◯	◯	◯
Bread, Cakes and Biscuits			◯	◯
Pastry and Pies		◯	◯	◯
Desserts	◯	◯	◯	◯
Ice Cream	◯		◯	

the sheet together above the food and fold them neatly downwards to bring the wrappings as close to the food as possible. Seal this fold, then fold ends like a parcel to make them close and tight, excluding air. Seal all folds and overwrap if necessary. This is sometimes called the 'druggist's wrap' or 'chemist's wrap'.

Bag Wrapping

Bags must be completely open before filling, and food must go down into corners, leaving no air pockets. A funnel is useful to avoid mess at the top of the bag. Bags can be sealed by heat or twist closing. For easier handling and storage, bags may be placed in other rigid containers for filling and freezing, then removed in a more compact form.

Heat Sealing

Polythene bags may be sealed by applying heat. This can be done with a special sealing iron or machine, but can also be handled with a domestic iron. When using a domestic iron, a thin strip of brown paper should be placed between the iron and the top of the polythene bag. It is important that all air should be excluded before sealing. Heat sealing gives a neat package which can be stored easily.

Twist Tying

All air should be extracted from the bag, and then a plastic-covered fastener twisted round the end of the bag. The top of the bag should then be turned down over this twist, and the fastener twisted again round the bunched neck of the bag. This gives a neat parcel, and ensures an airtight seal. It is sometimes known as a 'goose-neck closing'. Rubber bands are not recommended for this type of closing, as they perish at freezer temperatures.

Tape Sealing

Special freezer tape must be used. It should be applied to all containers with lids which do not have a special airtight seal, and to sheet-wrapped items. Tape should join the lid and container on cartons

Always ensure that bags containing sauces and purées are placed within plastic containers. The bags are easily sealed with a twist of these special wired strips.

Sheets of polythene film are the best way to wrap any awkward shaped foods for the freezer. Always label the foods clearly with the date of freezing so that you can easily estimate their freezer life.

It is well worth buying foil containers as they make packing any food simple, and because of their uniform shape they stack easily and economically inside the freezer.

and plastic boxes, with an additional piece of tape over the lid to reach down the sides. On sheet-wrapped items, all folds must be taped so that all air is excluded.

Brick Freezing

When a large quantity of liquid such as stock or soup has to be frozen, freezer space can be wasted by using irregularly shaped containers. It is most practical to freeze this type of liquid in 'brick' form. The liquid can be poured into loaf tins of a convenient size, frozen, removed from the containers, and wrapped in freezer foil or polythene for easy storage.

Ice Cube Freezing

The same method can be used for freezing small quantities of liquid such as concentrated soups, sauces, fruit and vegetable purées, leftover tea and coffee, herbs, syrups and juices. The liquid should be poured into the ice cube trays and frozen without covering. Each cube should then be wrapped in foil and packed in quantities in a polythene bag for easy storage. The cubes can also be sprayed with soda water and packed in bulk, and will not stick together. Each cube will generally be enough for a single serving of the food.

Labelling and Recording

All items in the freezer should be labelled carefully, as many frozen items look alike after storage, particularly meat. Label with the name of the food, size of package in portions or by weight, and date of freezing. If possible include the date by which food should be eaten. Add details of additional seasonings or other ingredients which must be added for serving, and of any planned accompaniments.

Labels must be written in felt pen, wax crayon or Chinagraph pencil, as other types of pen or pencil fade in the freezer. Labels can be written on tie-labels (which save additional closing wires), on labels treated with special adhesive which will stand sub-zero temperatures, or on paper tucked into transparent packages. It is easier to put stick-on labels on a package before filling it with food.

Recording

It is difficult to remember to keep records of food in

the freezer, but it is essential to maintain some sort of record so that food is used in rotation while it is still of high quality. A plastic shopping list which can be wiped clean is easy to use. A book or card index is more difficult to maintain regularly. Record the food frozen, the number and size of packages, the date of freezing, the date by which food should be eaten, and the number of packets removed.

Keeping the Freezer Tidy

It is much easier to use a freezer and maintain a regular turnover of food if the contents are kept tidy. An upright freezer is easier to organise because different shelves or drawers can be used for the various types of food. Avoid using cardboard boxes for storage as these take up a lot of space and become messy.

Baskets and Dividers

Plastic-covered wire mesh freezer baskets are available for hanging across the top of chest freezers and for use for stacking. Dividers are also available. This means that a main division can be made between meat and vegetables, for instance, or between raw materials and cooked foods.
NOTE: It must be remembered that baskets can be heavy to lift from the bottom of freezers when full of food.

Bags

Brightly-coloured mesh shopping bags are useful for keeping the freezer tidy. They can be filled with bag-wrapped food and with awkward-shaped parcels and are easy to lift. Large coloured polythene bags can also be used, but the contents are less easy to distinguish. Different colours of mesh or polythene bags can be used to identify types of food, such as fruit and vegetables.

Colour Coding

Identification of food can be greatly aided by using distinguishing colours. Bags, batching bags, labels and rigid boxes are available in six colours, so that one can identify different groups of food e.g. meat, vegetables, fruit; or a distinction can be made between different types of one food e.g. carrots, peas, beans.

Bulk Buying and Cooking

Bulk Buying

Most people assume that buying in bulk will lead to a considerable saving in the family budget. Savings depend however on the number of people in the family, shopping and eating habits and the accessibility of shops. Freezer owners in fact find that they save on such hidden factors as public transport fares, or petrol and parking charges for cars, and they save a great deal of shopping time (which represents money). They also find that, although their overall shopping bills may remain the same, they tend to live better, since the price of better cuts of meat or out-of-season vegetables is balanced by freezing cheaper meat or home produce.

Factors Affecting Bulk Buying

It is a mistake to buy in bulk with price as the only consideration. This can result in poor quality food. For instance a cheap bag of prawns will probably have come from warmer waters and be tasteless compared with cold-water prawns from Greenland or Norway which are initially more expensive. In fact, the customer usually gets exactly what he pays for, and quality rarely combines with cheapness. When choosing a source of supply for buying food in bulk, therefore, it is worth considering the quality of the food, the service offered and the amount of food to be bought at one time.

It is also important to know the storage capacity of the freezer, and to judge how much space will be taken up by bulk purchases, and a lot depends on the packaging and the shape of the food packages stored.

Some consideration must also be given to high quality storage life. There is little point in buying a large pack of fish fingers for instance, if the family cannot eat these up within three months, as quality, flavour and texture deteriorate when the recommended storage life is exceeded.

How to Buy in Bulk

(a) **Check on savings of time or money.** Before making out bulk orders, check how the family money is spent and where the greatest savings can be made. Some bulk purchases, such as meat, save money. Other purchases, such as bread, save time. Some families hate spending time on shopping or cooking; so these factors should be considered when choosing the types to buy in bulk.

(b) **Check on quality.** Test small quantities of food before placing a large order. It is expensive, in the long run, if a bulk order of meat pies turns out to be unpopular with the family after one has been eaten. The remaining pies will take up valuable freezer space, and may put the whole family off this type of frozen food for ever; little is lost by trying an individual item first.

Cheapness can also mean poor quality, so study order lists carefully. There may be many varieties of garden peas, for instance, and what looks like good value on paper can turn out to be very poor value indeed if the quality is low; much of the food may be wasted.

(c) **Check on packaging.** See that bulk food is properly packed for long-term storage. Food originally prepared for commercial and rapid use may come simply packed in cardboard boxes, or be slung into a polythene bag. A 7 lb/3·5 kg slab of pastry or 10 lb/5 kg minced meat clinging together in an enormous lump will be almost useless under home conditions. Be prepared to re-pack large purchases in usable quantities as soon as the food is purchased. Check also whether it will be more convenient and cheaper in the long run to buy a bulk quantity of individual or family-size portions rather than enormous packs which are difficult to handle and store.

Where to Buy in Bulk

(a) **Delivery Services.** Some frozen food manufacturers and some freezer centres deliver in bulk to the door. This is a convenient way of ordering food since it can be transferred straight from the refrigerated van to storage, and it is particularly useful in country areas. A minimum order is normally stipulated, and it is worth preparing a bulk order with friends to make the delivery a worthwhile business. Sample small quantities of items which have not been bought before, and check delivery lists carefully to see that the order has been properly filled.

(b) Frozen Food Centres. These are found in many towns, and are useful for buying a wide variety of foods in both family and commercial pack sizes. They are useful places for trying new items before placing bulk orders, and the customer has the advantage of seeing and comparing the types of food. Try to choose a centre which is near a good parking space, and from which food can be taken home quickly. It is better to stick to reputable shops where the turnover is quick and the storage conditions are good. Some centres buy mainly on price and quality may be poor. Try to find the best shopping day for freezer centres when they take their main deliveries. It is not always a good idea to shop at a freezer centre on a Friday or Saturday, when most other people are shopping; stocks of popular items may be low, so that a planned list cannot be completely filled and valuable shopping time is wasted. Check also on highly seasonal items, particularly fruit. Popular fruits such as redcurrants and raspberries tend to be in short supply after a while, so if the family likes them, stock up in the summer when first supplies come in, since these fruits have a long storage life.

(c) Specialist Producers. Meat in particular is sold by specialist producers, either frozen or prepared for freezing. Such firms operate delivery services or express postal services, or food can be collected. The quality is usually high.

(d) Local Shops, Markets and Farms. Local shops and markets can usually supply fruit by the case and vegetables by the sack at reduced rates, as can local growers. A check should be kept on quality, as food may remain in shops for some days before sale. It is not a good idea to buy in this way if time is short, as there is a lot of labour involved in preparing a sack of vegetables for the freezer. Farmers often supply vegetables, fruit, meat or poultry, and fruit or vegetables are often very cheap if picked by the customer. Fish and shellfish are worth buying direct from the boat or from a seaside shop which has daily supplies. Home-baked bread, cakes and pies can often be obtained from local shops, W.I. stalls, etc. and some housewives undertake bulk cooking for the freezer.

What to Buy in Bulk
All types of food can be bought in bulk, but there is skill in choosing foods which the family will like and eat in quantity, and in balancing the quantities and types of food to be stored. Some savings may be in time, while other savings will be directly financial.

Bread and Cakes
Considerable time is saved by buying baked goods in bulk. This is an opportunity to buy crusty loaves; bread made from special flours; rolls and baps; sliced loaves for sandwiches and toast; buns; crumpets; malt and fruit loaves and cakes.

Bread keeps well in the freezer and it is worth having a few fancy loaves in stock for special occasions.

Convenience Foods
Food which has been prepared to save cooking and serving time is useful for quick meals, and partilarly for in-between meals such as high tea for children which may not be required for the whole family. There are considerable savings in bulk packs of beefburgers, fish fingers, fishcakes, sausages, and thin cuts of meat and fish. Check the different kinds for variations in flavour and texture to see which are most popular with the family.

Prepared Dishes
Prepared pies, casseroles, puddings and gourmet dishes are useful for families which have little time for cooking. They should be bought in sizes most convenient for family use or for entertaining. Party dishes which need elaborate ingredients or lengthy cooking time are also useful. It is a good idea to buy small sizes first to see if they are acceptable.

Beef goulash is an ideal freezer dish to serve to unexpected visitors.
Fantasy sundaes can be quickly prepared with fresh or frozen fruit, ice-cream and whipped cream.

Fruit and Vegetables

Farm or market produce can be home-frozen but takes time for preparation. It may be more useful to buy commercially-frozen fruit and vegetables in large packs. Particularly useful are such items as chips, mushrooms, green and red peppers, onions and mixed casserole vegetables. These are all in constant use in the kitchen, but are not always on hand in an accessible shop; nor are they particularly easy to prepare for freezing at home. Small quantities for recipe use can be shaken out of loose-packed commercial bags.

Ice Cream

Ice cream in bulk containers is useful for a family of children. The quality soon deteriorates if a container is frequently opened and 'scooped', and the product has a relatively short high quality storage life, so it may be more practical to buy bulk supplies of smaller packs, or of individual ices such as lollies and chocolate bars which are easy to serve and have a longer storage life.

Poultry

Whole birds and poultry pieces are very useful for adding variety to family menus, and prices are usually reasonable. They are very useful for converting into cooked dishes for the freezer for both family use and entertaining. Some farms and shops prepare free-range birds in quantity for home-freezing; others supply commercially-frozen poultry in bulk. It is best to pack giblets and livers separately in bulk for the freezer, as they do not store well inside birds, and are useful on their own for many recipes.

Meat

Meat is usually the most expensive item in the family budget, and is one of the most useful raw materials to buy in bulk. Bulk meat needs careful buying, and it is worth studying the problems before making an expensive purchase.

It is usually most practical to buy enough meat for the family's needs for three months, which is a reasonable turnover time and about the cheapest length of time to store the meat, allowing for the running costs of a freezer. It is a great mistake to purchase a quarter of beef, a pig and a lamb all at the same time, as novice freezer-owners tend to do. This overloads the freezer at the expense of other items, and pork in particular may deteriorate if kept beyond the recommended high quality storage life period. It is better to combine with one or two other families to get the advantage of bulk purchase with a variety of types of meat and different cuts.

Whole carcasses are ideal for those who will cook and eat cheaper cuts. Otherwise these will be wasted, and the roasting and grilling cuts will prove more expensive in the end. If a family only likes the better cuts, it is better to make a bulk purchase of these, or to buy a good variety pack of different meats. There will not be much financial saving, but there will be shopping convenience and no wastage. In bulk carcass buying, there may be considerable wastage in bones and suet; prices must be checked carefully to be sure the actual price of the meat used is not in excess of that quoted by the supplier.

Many experts do not recommend the home-freezing of meat at all. This is because meat must be frozen very quickly to retain its high quality, and commercial blast-freezing techniques give better results. If you do freeze meat at home, it is important

Different foods are easily identified in the freezer if you use clear-wrap or these clear-fronted foil packs which are especially good for individual items like these single pork chops.

Roast veal stuffed with kidneys is accompanied here by French beans, cauliflower and baby tomatoes.

to set the freezer correctly and only to freeze the recommended quantities at one time, and to label meat very carefully with the name of the cut and its possible uses. It is often better to choose the meat and have it frozen by the supplier. This does not apply, of course, to home-killed meat, or home-caught game and fish.

When buying meat, choose good quality, and see that it has been properly hung. See also that a list is made of all the cuts in the order and their possible uses (see tables for cuts of meat on pages 47–8), and also that they are packed in usable quantities. Get the meat properly prepared in the form in which it is wanted, either joints, steaks, casserole meat or mince. These specific points on our four principal meats are worth noting:

(a) Beef is a really bulky purchase. A forequarter will account for about 100 lb/45 kg and a hind-quarter is even larger. The forequarter is more manageable, but consists mainly of slow-cooking cuts. Boned joints take up far less space in the freezer. The bones will account for about one-quarter of a bulk purchase, but can be made into concentrated stock for freezing (the butcher should be asked to saw them in reasonable pieces for the saucepan). Suet can be used for a wide variety of puddings, and can also be rendered down for fat. Check whether bones and suet are included in the overall price and if they will be delivered with the meat. Have the slow-cooking meat cut into slices and/or cubes for easy use, and ask for plenty of lean mince in 1 lb/450 g packs which are very useful. Try to convert some of the cuts straight into pies or casseroles when they are delivered; this will save freezer space and provide some useful meals for quick use.

(b) Veal is not very often available in bulk, and is not very successful in the freezer, since it tends to lose flavour in storage conditions. If veal is bought, see that it is carefully divided into prepared boned roasting joints, escalopes and chops, and pie veal, etc.

(c) Lamb is worth buying. A small lean one will weigh 25–30 lb/12–14 kg with little waste. Decide if you want chops in roasting joints or divided. If the cheaper chops and breast of lamb are not liked, it may be better value simply to buy roasting joints and bags of chops.

(d) Pork has a shorter storage life than other meats and should not be purchased in over-large quantities. Half a pig will weigh about 50 lb/22 kg and consists mostly of roasting and frying joints. The head and trotters may be included, but freezer space should not be wasted on them. They are better used at once in brawn or a dish which requires meat jelly.

Bulk Cooking

It can be all too easy to become a slave to the freezer, endlessly shopping and cooking to keep the white box topped up. It is important to take advantage of the fact that this is the only way of safely preserving cooked dishes. Cooking should be organised ahead so that two or three ready meals are always 'in hand' in the freezer. The great thing is to avoid inflicting the same kind of food on the family for weeks ahead, so new bulk purchases should be slightly different from the one recently made, and the cooked dishes used to vary those already in hand.

One of the greatest advantages of bulk cooking is that quantities of raw materials, such as bulk-bought meat, can be converted into cooked dishes as soon as they have been bought, saving considerable space. Stewing steak, for instance, can be made into casseroles and pies; mince can be converted into individual pies and shepherd's pies; chicken pieces can be used with a whole variety of sauces; offal can be made into casseroles and pâtés.

For most people, it is best to double or treble quantities of such dishes as casseroles, using one immediately and saving the other portions for future use with added seasonings. Batch-baking is also sensible, to take full advantage of oven heat. It takes little more effort to make two cakes instead of one, fifty scones instead of ten. The same goes for pâtés, ice creams etc.

The Right Equipment

It pays to have the right-sized equipment and one or two labour-saving machines to use in conjunction with the freezer. Normal household equipment may not be suitable for bulk cooking.

Roast lamb makes a good meal all the year round and may be flavoured with rosemary or mint.

(a) Large saucepans are useful not only for making stock, but for blanching vegetables and preparing fruit and meat. A large flat pan is useful for cooking ingredients in fat at the first stage of many recipes.

(b) Large casseroles are another essential. At least one 6–8 pint/3–4 litre size is needed for bulk cooking, or a large double roaster.

(c) A pressure cooker speeds up the cooking of meat and poultry in particular. It can also double as an ordinary large pan.

(d) An electric mixer with attachments is invaluable in cooking for the freezer. The mixer itself is useful for making all types of cakes, and for beating ice cream and whipping up puddings. The blender attachment, or an independent blender, is useful for soups, purées and sauces. A mincer attachment aids the making of mince and sausages from bulk-bought meat, and speeds up pâté-making. A slicing attachment is handy for preparing vegetables, and a dough-hook is useful for yeast doughs for bread, buns and pizzas.

An adequate oven is necessary to take batch-baking, etc. If a new one is being purchased, see that there is plenty of oven space, and if possible buy a cooker with a fan-assisted oven. This ensures that heat is circulated and a steady baking temperature is maintained throughout the oven. Cooks who have an Aga or similar stove with two ovens are fortunate, as different types of dishes can be cooked at the same time.

What to cook for freezing Before cooking foods for freezing, it is wise to assess which items are worth freezer space. Briefly, these are:

(a) Dishes which need long cooking or long and tedious preparation.

(b) Dishes made from seasonal foods.

(c) Dishes which can be made in large quantities with little more work (i.e. three cakes instead of one; double or treble casseroles).

(d) Dishes for special occasions, such as parties or holidays.

(e) Convenience foods for invalids, small children, unexpected illness.

Freezing Vegetables and Herbs

All vegetables to be frozen should be young and tender, and they are best picked and frozen in small amounts. Shop-bought vegetables are generally too old to be worth freezing, but a few seasonal delicacies such as aubergines and peppers are worth the trouble of preparing them.

Vegetables to be frozen must be blanched to arrest the working of enzymes (types of protein in foods which speed up chemical reactions). Blanching at high heat stops the enzymes from affecting quality, flavour, colour and nutritive value during storage. Unblanched vegetables can be stored for up to three months in the freezer, but the effect of freezing will be the same as that of an early frost, and they will lose their colour and texture. Unblanched vegetables also require the full cooking time, unlike blanched vegetables which are already partly cooked.

Preparation for Freezing
All vegetables must first be washed thoroughly in cold water, then cut or sorted into similar sizes. If more are picked than can be dealt with, they should be put into polythene bags in a refrigerator.

Blanching
There are two forms of blanching, (a) by water; (b) by steam. Steam blanching is not recommended for leafy green vegetables which tend to mat together, and it takes longer than water blanching, though it conserves more minerals and vitamins. Blanching should be timed carefully, though inaccuracy will not be disastrous. Too little blanching may result in colour change and in a loss of nutritive value; too much blanching will mean a loss of crispness and fresh flavour.
(a) Water blanching. Blanch only 1 lb/450 g vegetables at a time to ensure thoroughness and to prevent a quick change in the temperature of the water. Use a saucepan holding at least 8 pints/4 litres of water. Bring the water to the boil while the vegetables are being prepared. Put vegetables into a wire basket, chip pan, salad shaker or a muslin bag and completely immerse in the saucepan of fast-boiling water; cover tightly and keep the heat high under the saucepan until blanching is completed. Check carefully the time needed for each vegetable (see below, pages 27–34) and time blanching from when water returns to boiling point. As soon as the full blanching time has elapsed, remove vegetables and drain at once. Bring water to boiling point again before dealing with another batch of vegetables.
(b) Steam blanching. Put enough water into the saucepan below a steamer to prevent any risk of it boiling dry. Prepare the vegetables, and when the water is boiling fast put the wire basket or muslin bag into steamer. Cover tightly, and count steaming time from when the steam escapes from the lid. Steam blanching takes half as long again as water blanching (e.g. 2 minutes water blanching equals 3 minutes steam blanching).

Cooling
Cooling must be done immediately after blanching, and it must be very thorough indeed; before being packed for the freezer, the vegetables should be cool right through to the centre. The time taken is generally equal to the blanching time if a large quantity of cold water is used. It is best to ice-chill this water, and it is a good idea to prepare large quantities of ice the day before a vegetable freezing session is planned. Vegetables which are not cooled quickly become mushy as they will go on cooking in their own heat. After cooling in the water, the vegetables should be thoroughly drained, and preferably finished off on absorbent paper.

Packing
Pack the cooled food in usable quantities to suit family or entertaining needs (see above, page 24). Vegetables can be packed in bags or boxes; the

chosen method will depend on the storage space available, as bagged vegetables are more difficult to keep though obviously cheaper to prepare.

Vegetables are normally packed dry, though wet-packing in brine is believed to prevent the vegetables toughening in storage, and non-leafy varieties can be packed in this way. The vegetables are packed into rigid containers to within 1 in/2·5 cm of the top, and are then just covered with brine, made in the proportion of 2 tablespoons salt per 2 pints/1 litre water, leaving ½ in/1·25 cm headspace. It may be found in hard water areas that home-frozen vegetables are consistently tough, and it is then worth experimenting with this brine method.

Cooking

The best results are obtained from cooking vegetables immediately on removal from the freezer. When cooking unthawed vegetables, break the blocks into 4 or 5 pieces when removing from the carton, to allow heat to penetrate evenly and rapidly.

One or two vegetables such as broccoli and spinach are better cooked partially thawed, and corn on the cob needs complete thawing. Mushrooms should be cooked frozen; they become pulpy when thawed. If vegetables are thawed, they should be cooked at once.

Partial cooking during blanching, and the tenderising process produced by temperature changes during storage, reduce the final cooking time of frozen vegetables. In general, they should cook in one-third to one-half the time allowed for fresh vegetables. Very little water, if any, should be used for cooking frozen vegetables; about ¼ pint/125 ml to 1 lb/450 g vegetables, depending on variety, is plenty. The water should be boiling, the vegetables covered at once with a lid, and as soon as boiling point is reached again, the vegetables should be simmered gently for the required time. Since flavour is always lost into the cooking water, some cooks prefer to steam vegetables, cook them in a double boiler, or to bake or fry them. For baking, the vegetables should be separated and drained, then put into a greased casserole with a knob of butter and seasoning, covered tightly and baked at 350°F/180°C/Gas Mark 4 for about 30 minutes. For frying, the vegetables remain frozen, and are put into a heavy frying pan containing 1 oz/25 g melted butter. The pan must be tightly covered and the vegetables cooked gently until they separate, then cooked over moderate heat until cooked through and tender, being turned as required to prevent burning.

Here are notes on preparing, packing, storing and cooking various kinds of vegetables. The blanching times given are for water blanching:

Asparagus

Artichokes (Globe)
Preparation
(a) Remove outer leaves. Wash, trim stalks and remove 'chokes'. Blanch in 8 pints/5 litres water with 1 tablespoon lemon juice for 7 minutes. Cool and drain upside down. Pack in boxes.
(b) Remove all green leaves and 'chokes'. Blanch artichoke hearts for 5 minutes.
To serve
(a) Cook in boiling water for 5 minutes. (b) Use as fresh artichokes for special dishes.
High Quality Storage Life (a) 12 months, (b) 12 months

Artichokes (Jerusalem)
Preparation
Peel and cut in slices. Soften in a little butter, and simmer in a chicken stock. Rub through a sieve and pack in boxes.
To serve
Use as a basis for soup with milk or cream and seasoning.
High Quality Storage Life 3 months

Asparagus
Preparation
Wash and remove woody portions and scales. Grade for size and cut in 6 in/15 cm lengths. Blanch 2 minutes (small spears); 3 minutes (medium spears); 4 minutes (large spears). Cool and drain. Pack in boxes.
To serve
Cook 5 minutes in boiling water.
High Quality Storage Life 9 months

Aubergines

Preparation

Use mature, tender, medium-sized.

(a) Peel and cut in 1 in/2·5 cm slices. Blanch 4 minutes, chill and drain. Pack in layers separated by paper in boxes. (b) Coat slices in thin batter, or egg and breadcrumbs. Deep-fry, drain and cool. Pack in layers in boxes.

To serve

(a) Cook 5 minutes in boiling water, (b) Heat in a slow oven or part-thaw and deep-fry.

High Quality Storage Life (a) 12 months, (b) 1 month

Beans (Broad)

Preparation

Use small young beans. Shell and blanch for $1\frac{1}{2}$ minutes. Pack in bags or boxes.

To serve

Cook 8 minutes in boiling water.

High Quality Storage Life 12 months

Beans (French)

Preparation

Remove tops and tails. Leave small beans whole; cut larger ones into 1 in/2·5 cm pieces. Blanch 3 minutes (whole beans); 2 minutes (cut beans). Cool and pack in bags.

To serve

Cook 7 minutes in boiling water (whole beans); 5 minutes (cut beans).

High Quality Storage Life 12 months

Beans (Runner)

Preparation

Do not shred, but cut in pieces and blanch 2 minutes. Cool and pack.

To serve

Cook 7 minutes in boiling water.

High Quality Storage Life 12 months

Beetroot

Preparation

Use very young beetroot, under 3 in/7·5 cm across. Cook in boiling water until tender. Rub off skins and pack in boxes, either whole or cut in slices.

To serve

Thaw 2 hours in container in refrigerator. Drain and add dressing.

High Quality Storage Life 6 months

Broccoli

Preparation

Use green, compact heads with tender stalks 1 in/2·5 cm thick or less. Trim stalks and remove outer leaves. Wash well and soak in salt water for 30 minutes (2 teaspoons salt to 8 pints/5 litres water). Wash in fresh water, and cut into sprigs. Blanch 3 minutes (thin stems); 4 minutes (5 minutes thick stems). Pack into boxes or bags, alternating heads.

To serve

Cook 8 minutes in boiling water.

High Quality Storage Life 12 months

Brussels Sprouts

Preparation

Grade small compact heads. Clean and wash well. Blanch 3 minutes (small); 4 minutes (medium). Cool and pack in bags or boxes.

To serve

Cook 8 minutes in boiling water.

High Quality Storage Life 12 months

Cabbage (Green and Red)

Preparation

Use crisp young cabbage. Wash and shred finely. Blanch $1\frac{1}{2}$ minutes. Pack in bags.

To serve

Cook 8 minutes in boiling water. Do not use raw.

High Quality Storage Life 6 months

Carrots

Preparation

Use very young carrots. Wash and scrape. Blanch 3 minutes for small whole carrots, sliced or diced carrots. Pack in bags or boxes.

To serve

Cook 8 minutes in boiling water.

High Quality Storage Life 12 months

Carrots

28

Cauliflower

Preparation

Use firm compact heads with close white flowers. Wash and break into sprigs. Blanch 3 minutes in 8 pints/5 litres water with 1 tablespoon lemon juice. Cool and pack in lined boxes or bags.

To serve

Cook 10 minutes in boiling water.

High Quality Storage Life   6 months

Celery

Preparation

(a) Use crisp young stalks. Scrub well and remove strings. Cut in 1 in/2·5 cm lengths and blanch 2 minutes. Cool and drain and pack in bags.

(b) Prepare as above, but pack in boxes with water used for blanching, leaving ½ in headspace.

To serve

Use as a vegetable, or for stews or soups, using liquid if available. Do not use raw.

High Quality Storage Life   6 months

Chestnuts

Preparation

Bring chestnuts in shells to the boil. Drain and peel off shells. Pack in boxes or bags.

To serve

Cook in boiling water or milk, according to recipe.

High Quality Storage Life   6 months

Chicory

Preparation

Wash well and remove outer leaves. Blanch 3 minutes and cool in cooking liquid. Pack in the blanching liquid in boxes, leaving ½ in/1·25 cm headspace.

To serve

Put into a covered dish in the oven in blanching liquid and heat at 350°F/180°C/Gas Mark 4 for 40 minutes. Drain and serve with butter.

High Quality Storage Life   6 months

Corn-on-the-Cob

Preparation

(a) Use fresh tender corn. Remove leaves and threads and grade cobs for size. Blanch 4 minutes (small cobs); 6 minutes (medium cobs); 8 minutes (large cobs). Cool and dry. Pack individually in foil or freezer paper. Freeze and pack in bags.

(b) Blanch cobs and scrape off kernels. Pack in boxes, leaving ½ in/1·25 cm headspace.

To serve

(a) Thaw before cooking. Put cobs in cold water, bring to a fast boil and simmer 5 minutes.

(b) Thaw in wrappings in refrigerator. Cook 10 minutes in boiling water.

High Quality Storage Life   12 months

Sweet Corn

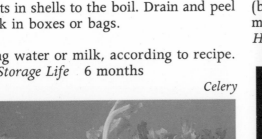

Celery

Cucumber

Preparation

Cut in thin slices and pack in boxes. Cover with equal quantities white vinegar and water, seasoned with ½ teaspoon sugar and 1 teaspoon black pepper to 1 pint/500 ml liquid.

To serve

Thaw in container in refrigerator. Drain and season with salt.

High Quality Storage Life   2 months

Fennel

Preparation

Use crisp young stalks. Scrub well. Blanch 3 minutes. Cool and pack in blanching water in boxes.

To serve

Simmer 30 minutes in blanching water or stock. Slip hard cores from roots when cooked.

High Quality Storage Life   6 months

Fennel

Herbs (Mint, Parsley and Chives)

Preparation

(a) Wash and pack sprigs in bags.

(b) Chop finely and pack into ice-cube trays. Transfer frozen cubes to bags for storage.

To serve

Thaw at room temperature for sandwich fillings. Add cubes to sauces, soups or stews. Do not use for garnish as they become limp.

High Quality Storage Life   6 months

Kale

Preparation

Use young, tender kale. Remove dry or tough leaves. Strip leaves from stems and blanch 1 minute Cool and drain. Chop leaves for convenient packing. Pack into bags.

To serve

Cook 8 minutes in boiling water.

High Quality Storage Life   6 months

Kohlrabi

Preparation

Use young and tender, not too large, and mild-flavoured. Trim, wash and peel. Small ones may be frozen whole, but large ones should be diced. Blanch 3 minutes (whole); 2 minutes (diced). Cool and pack in bags or boxes.

To serve

Cook 10 minutes in boiling water.

High Quality Storage Life   12 months

Leeks

Leeks

Preparation

Trim off roots and green stems. Wash very well and remove dirty outer layers. Cut either finely or coarsely into even lengths. Blanch finely-cut leeks for 1½ minutes; coarsely-cut leeks for 3 minutes. Cool thoroughly and drain, or pack in blanching liquid.

To serve

Cook drained leeks until tender in salted water, and serve with butter or sauce, or make into a purée, or add to a soup or stew. Leeks packed in blanching liquid can be used to make soup.

High Quality Storage Life   12 months

Marrow

Preparation

(a) Cut young marrows or courgettes in ½ in/1·25 cm slices without peeling. Blanch 3 minutes and pack in boxes, leaving ½ in/1·25 cm headspace. (b) Peel and seed large marrows. Cook until soft, mash and pack in boxes.

To serve

(a) Fry in oil, and season well. (b) Reheat in double boiler with butter and seasoning.

High Quality Storage Life   6 months

Courgettes

Mushrooms

Preparation

(a) Wipe but do not peel. Cut large mushrooms in slices. Stalks may be frozen separately. Blanch 1½ minutes in 6 pints/3 litres water with 1 tablespoon lemon juice. Pack cups down in boxes, leaving 1½ in /3·75 cm headspace. (b) Grade and cook in butter for 5 minutes. Allow 6 tablespoons butter to 1 lb/450 g mushrooms. Cool quickly, take off excess fat, and pack in boxes.

To serve

(a) Thaw in container in refrigerator, and cook in butter. (b) Add while frozen to soups, stews or other dishes.

High Quality Storage Life   (a) 3 months, (b) 2 months

Onions

Onions

Preparation

(a) Peel, chop and pack in small boxes. Overwrap. (b) Cut in slices and wrap in foil or freezer paper, dividing layers with paper. Overwrap. (c) Chop or slice, blanch 2 minutes. Cool and drain. Pack in boxes. Overwrap. (d) Leave tiny onions whole. Blanch 4 minutes. Pack in boxes. Overwrap.

To serve

Thaw raw onions in refrigerator. Add to salads while frosty. Add frozen onions to dishes according to recipe.

High Quality Storage Life   2 months

Parsnips

Preparation

Use young parsnips. Trim and peel. Cut into narrow strips or dice. Blanch 2 minutes. Pack in bags or boxes.

To serve

Cook 15 minutes in boiling water.

High Quality Storage Life   12 months

Peas, Green

Preparation

Use young sweet peas. Shell. Blanch 1 minute, shaking basket to distribute heat. Cool and drain. Pack in boxes or bags.

To serve

Cook 7 minutes in boiling water.

High Quality Storage Life   12 months

Peas (Edible Pods)

Preparation

Use flat tender pods. Wash well. Remove ends and strings. Blanch ½ minute in small quantities.

To serve

Cook 7 minutes in boiling water.

High Quality Storage Life   12 months

Peas

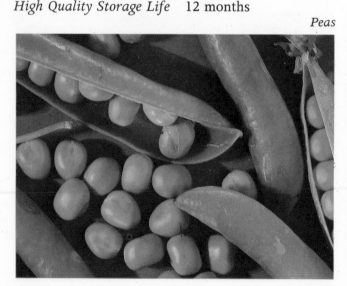

Peppers (Green and Red)

Preparation

(a) Wash well. Cut off stems and caps, and remove seeds and membranes. Blanch 2 minutes (slices); 3 minutes (halves). Pack in boxes or bags. (b) Grill on high heat until skin is charred. Plunge into cold water and rub off skins. Remove caps and seeds. Pack tightly in boxes in salt solution (1 tablespoon salt to 1 pint/500 ml water), leaving 1 in/2·5 cms headspace.

To serve

(a) Thaw 1½ hours at room temperature. (b) Thaw in liquid and drain. Dress with oil and seasoning.

High Quality Storage Life   12 months

Peppers

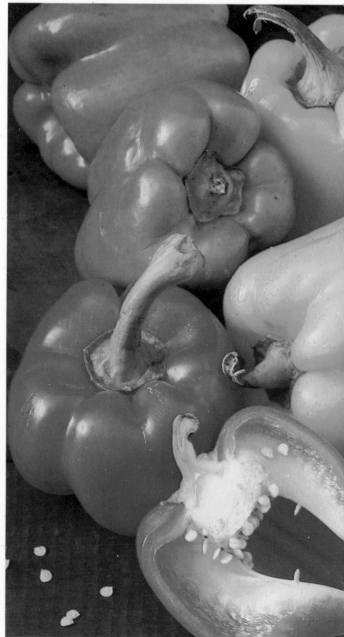

Potatoes

Preparation

(a) Scrape and wash new potatoes. Blanch 4 minutes. Cool and pack in bags. (b) Slightly undercook new potatoes. Drain, toss in butter, cool and pack in bags. (c) Mash potatoes with butter and hot milk. Pack in boxes or bags. (d) Form potatoes into croquettes or Duchesse Potatoes. Cook, cool and pack in boxes. (e) Fry chips in clean fat for 4 minutes. Do not brown. Cool and pack in bags.

To serve

(a) Cook 15 minutes in boiling water. (b) Plunge bag in boiling water. Take off heat and leave 10 minutes. (c) Reheat in double boiler. (d) Thaw 2 hours. Heat at 350°F/180°C/Gas Mark 4 for 20 minutes. (e) Fry in deep fat.

High Quality Storage Life (a) 12 months, (b) 3 months, (c) 3 months, (d) 3 months, (e) 3 months

Potato chips may be frozen but they must be blanched in oil before packing.

Pumpkin

Pumpkin

Preparation

Peel and seed. Cook until soft. Mash and pack in boxes.

To serve

(a) Reheat in double boiler with butter and seasoning. (b) Thaw 2 hours at room temperature and use as a pie filling.

High Quality Storage Life 6 months

Spinach

Preparation

Use young tender spinach. Remove stems. Wash very well. Blanch 2 minutes, shaking basket so the leaves separate. Cool and press out moisture. Pack in boxes or bags.

To serve

Melt a little butter and cook frozen spinach 7 minutes.

High Quality Storage Life 12 months

Tomatoes

Preparation

(a) Wipe tomatoes and remove stems. Grade and pack in small quantities in bags. (b) Skin and core tomatoes. Simmer in own juice for 5 minutes until soft. Sieve, cool and pack in boxes. (c) Core tomatoes and cut in quarters. Simmer with lid on for 10 minutes. Put through muslin. Cool juice and pack in boxes, leaving 1 in/2·5 cm headspace.

To serve

(a) Thaw 2 hours at room temperature, skins slip off when thawed. Grill, or use in recipes. Do not use raw. (b) Thaw 2 hours at room temperature. Use for soups or stews. (c) Thaw in refrigerator. Serve frosty. Add seasoning.

High Quality Storage Life 12 months

Tomatoes

Turnips

Preparation

(a) Use small, young mild turnips. Peel and cut in dice. Blanch $2\frac{1}{2}$ minutes. Cool and pack in boxes. (b) Cook turnips until tender. Drain and mash. Pack in boxes, leaving $\frac{1}{2}$ in/1·25 cm headspace.

To serve

(a) Cook 10 minutes in boiling water. (b) Reheat in double boiler with butter and seasoning.

High Quality Storage Life (a) 12 months, (b) 3 months

Vegetable Purée

Preparation

Cook and sieve vegetables. Pack in boxes. Small quantities can be frozen in ice-cube trays, and the cubes transferred to bags for easy storage.

To serve

Add to soups. Purée may be reheated in a double boiler.

High Quality Storage Life 3 months

Vegetables in Sauce

Preparation

Slightly undercook vegetables. Cool and fold into sauce. Pack into boxes.

To serve

Reheat in double boiler.

High Quality Storage Life 2 months

Vegetables (Mixed)

Preparation

Prepare and blanch vegetables separately. Mix and pack in boxes.

To serve

Cook 7 minutes in boiling water.

High Quality Storage Life 12 months

Freezing Fruit

The best results are obtained from fully-flavoured fruits, particularly berries. The blander fruits such as pears are satisfactory, but have little flavour. In general, fruit for freezing should be of top quality; over-ripe fruit will be mushy (though it may be possible to store as purée); unripe fruit will be tasteless and poorly-coloured.

It is important to work quickly when preparing fruit; home-picked fruit should be frozen on the same day, while fruit from shop or market should only be bought in manageable quantities which can be handled in a short space of time.

Whichever method of packing is to be used, wash the fruit in plenty of water containing ice cubes as this will prevent the fruit becoming soggy and losing juice. Fruit should be drained immediately in an enamel, aluminium, stainless steel or earthenware container (avoid copper, iron and galvanised ware which produce off-flavours), and may be further drained on absorbent paper. It is important to be gentle in removing stems or stones from fruit to be frozen; this should be done with the tips of the fingers, without squeezing.

Fruit Freezing Methods

Unsweetened Dry Pack

This pack can be used for fruit for use in pies, puddings and jams, or for people on a sugar-free diet. It should not be used for fruit which discolours badly during preparation, as sugar helps to retard the action of the enzymes which cause darkening.

To pack fruit by this method, wash and drain and pack into cartons. Do not use excess water in cleaning the fruit. Seal and freeze and label carefully. For an unsweetened pack, it is even better to open-freeze fruit. Spread it out on metal or plastic trays for fast-freezing. When frozen, pour into polythene bags or boxes for storage. Small quantities can easily be shaken out for use.

Unsweetened Wet Pack

This method is little used, but is acceptable for very sweet fruit or for puddings to be made for people on a diet. The fruit should be packed in liquid-proof containers, either gently crushed in its own juice, or covered with water to which lemon juice has been added to prevent discolouration (juice of 1 lemon to $1\frac{1}{2}$ pints/750 ml water). If the fruit is tart but no sugar is to be used, it may be frozen in water sweetened with a sugar substitute, or with a sugar-free carbonated beverage. Seal, freeze and label carefully.

Dry Sugar Pack

This is a good method for crushed or sliced fruit, or for soft juicy fruit from which the juice draws easily such as berries. The fruit should be washed and drained and may be packed by two methods: (a) mix fruit and sugar in a bowl with a silver spoon, adjusting sweetening to tartness of fruit (average 3 lb/$1\frac{1}{2}$ kg fruit to 1 lb/450 g sugar). Pack fruit into containers, leaving $\frac{1}{2}$ in/1·25 cm headspace, seal and freeze, and label carefully: (b) pack fruit in layers, using the same proportion of fruit and sugar; start with a layer of fruit, sprinkle with sugar, then more fruit and sugar, leaving $\frac{1}{2}$ in/1·25 cm headspace. Seal and freeze, labelling carefully.

Syrup Pack

This method is best for non-juicy fruits, and those which discolour easily. Syrup is normally made from white sugar and water. (For those who dislike white sugar for dietary reasons, honey may be used, but it flavours the fruit strongly. Brown sugar may likewise be used, but affects the colour of the fruit.)

The syrup is referred to as a percentage, according to the amount of sugar and water used. A medium syrup or 40% syrup is best for most purposes as a heavier syrup tends to make the fruit flabby. The sugar must be completely dissolved in boiling water, then cooled. It must be completely cold before adding it to the fruit, and it is best stored in a refrigerator for a day before using. The fruit should be packed into containers and covered with syrup, leaving $\frac{1}{2}$–1 in/1·25–2·5 cm headspace. To prevent discolouration, a piece of Cellophane should be pressed down over the fruit into the syrup before sealing, freezing and labelling.

SYRUP		
SUGAR	WATER	TYPE OF SYRUP
4 oz/100 g	1 pint/500 ml 20%	very light surup
7 oz/175 g	1 pint/500 ml 30%	light syrup
11 oz/325 g	1 pint/500 ml 40%	medium syrup
16 oz/450 g	1 pint/500 ml 50%	heavy syrup
25 oz/650 g	1 pint/500 ml 60%	very heavy syrup

Headspace

Headspace must be allowed for all fruit in sugar or syrup, for juice or purée: $\frac{1}{2}$ in/1·25 cm should be allowed for all dry packs; $\frac{1}{2}$–1 in/1·25–2·5 cm per pint/500 ml for wide-topped wet packs and $\frac{3}{4}$–1 in/2–2·5 cm per pint/500 ml for narrow-topped wet packs. Double headspace is needed for 2 pint/1 litre containers.

Discolouration

Discolouration is the greatest problem in fruit packing for freezing. Apples, peaches and pears are particularly subject to this during preparation, storage and thawing. In general, fruit which has a lot of Vitamin C darkens less easily, so adding lemon juice or citric acid to the sugar pack will help to arrest darkening. Use the juice of 1 lemon to $1\frac{1}{2}$ pints/750 ml water, or 1 teaspoon citric acid to each 1 lb/450 g sugar in dry pack. Ascorbic acid can likewise be used; it can be bought in tablet or crystalline form from the chemist. 500 milligrammes or 1 tablet of ascorbic acid should be used for 1 pint/500 ml water (1 teaspoon of the acid equals 6 tablets). The tablets should be crushed to a powder and mixed in a teaspoon of cold water before being added to the sugar syrup. Fruit purée in particular is subject to darkening since large amounts of air are forced through a sieve during preparation. Air reacts on the cells of fruit to produce darkening; and for this reason fruit should be prepared quickly for freezing once the natural protection of skin or rind is broken. For the same reason, the fruit should be eaten immediately on thawing, or while a few ice crystals remain. Fruit which discolours badly is better for rapid thawing, and unsweetened frozen fruit should immediately be put into hot syrup or other liquid.

Jam Fruit
Any fruit can be packed for use in jam-making later. Pack without sweetening, and allow 10% extra fruit in the recipe when making the jam, as there is a slight pectin loss in frozen fruit.

Fruit Purée
It is useful to freeze purée for certain kinds of puddings and cakes, and when there is a lot of ripe fruit. The fruit should not be over-ripe or bruised. Raw fruit such as raspberries or strawberries should be sieved, to remove all the pips. Other fruit can be put in a covered dish in the oven to start the juice running before the fruit is sieved. Purée can be made from cooked fruit but must be well cooled before freezing (it will keep less than 4 months). This purée should be sweetened, as if for immediate use. Ways of preparing purée from individual fruits are given under the individual fruits below.

Fruit Syrups
Fruit syrups can be frozen; blackcurrant is thought best, and it is far easier to freeze than to bottle. Any standard syrup recipe can be used, and fruit syrup is best frozen in small quantities in ice-cube trays. Each cube should be wrapped in foil; then, a useful number of cubes are packed into a bag for storage. One syrup cube gives one individual serving to use with puddings or ice cream, or to dissolve in water as a drink.

Fruit Juices
Ripe fruit can be turned into juice, and frozen in this form. Citrus fruit juice can also be frozen. Non-citrus fruit should be carefully checked for any bruising or insects, then mashed with a silver fork. For every 4 cups of fruit, allow 1 cup of water and simmer gently for 10 minutes. Strain through a jelly bag or cloth, and cool completely before freezing. These juices can be frozen unsweetened, or sweetened to taste, and are useful for drinks, jellies and fruit pies. Freeze them in a rigid container, leaving $\frac{1}{2}$ in/1·25 cm headspace, or in ice-cube trays, wrapping each cube in foil and storing in quantities in polythene bags. Apple juice can be made, using $\frac{1}{2}$ pint/250 ml water to each 2 lb/1 kg apples, or it can be made by simmering leftover peelings in water; it should *not* be sweetened before freezing since fermentation sets in quickly.

Citrus fruit juices can easily be prepared from good-quality fruit which is heavy in the hand for its size. The unpeeled fruit should be chilled in iced water or in the refrigerator before the juice is

extracted; the juice can be strained, but the fine pulp can be left in if preferred. Freeze in rigid containers, leaving 1 in/2·5 cm headspace. Lemon and lime juice can usefully be frozen in ice-cube trays for drinks, the cubes being wrapped in foil and stored in useful quantities in polythene bags.

Catering Packs of Fruit and Juice
Large tins of fruit in syrup and of fruit juices are often economical to buy. They can be opened and divided into normal family portions, and then be frozen in smaller containers.

Thawing Frozen Fruit
Unsweetened fruit packs take longer to thaw than sweetened ones; fruit in dry sugar thaws most quickly of all. All fruit should be thawed in its container, unopened; and all fruit is at its best when just thawed, with a few ice crystals left if it is to be eaten raw. Fruit to use with ice cream should only be partly defrosted. To cook frozen fruit, thaw until pieces can just be separated and put into a pie; if fruit is to be cooked in a saucepan, it can be put into the pan in its frozen state, keeping in mind the amount of sugar or syrup used earlier in freezing if a pudding is being made. Frozen fruits are likely to have a lot of juice after thawing; to avoid leaky pies or damp cake fillings, add a little thickening for pies (such as cornflour, arrowroot or flake tapioca), or drain off excess juice. For every 1 lb/450 g fruit

Fruit juices and syrups are an excellent base for milk shakes.

OVERLEAF: *Fresh fruit can be frozen, in season, to make a wide variety of delicious fruit salads throughout the year.*

packed in syrup, allow 6–8 hours thawing time in the refrigerator, 2–4 hours thawing at room temperature, or $\frac{1}{2}$–1 hour if the pack is placed in a bowl of cold water.

Fruit will lose quality and flavour if left to stand for any length of time after thawing, so do not thaw more than you need immediately. However, if left-over fruit is cooked, it will last for several days in a refrigerator.

Here are notes on preparing, packing, storing and cooking various fruits:

Apples
Preparation
Peel, core and drop in cold water. Cut in twelfths or sixteenths. Pack in bags or boxes. (a) Dry sugar pack (8 oz/225 g sugar to 2 lb/1 kg fruit). (b) 40% syrup pack. (c) Sweetened purée.
To serve
(a) Use for pies and puddings. (c) Use for sauce, fools and ices.
High Quality Storage Life (a) 8–12 months, (c) 4–8 months

Apricots
Preparation
(a) Peeled and halved in dry sugar pack (4 oz/100 g

Cherries

to 1 lb/450 g fruit) or 40% syrup pack. (b) Peeled and sliced in 40% syrup pack. (c) Sweetened purée (very ripe fruit).

To serve
(a) Thaw $3\frac{1}{2}$ hours at room temperature. (b) Use for sauce, and ices.
High Quality Storage Life (a) 12 months, (c) 4 months

Avocado Pears
Preparation
(a) Rub halves in lemon juice, wrap in foil and pack in polythene bags. (b) Dip slices in lemon juice and freeze in boxes. (c) Mash pulp with lemon juice (1 tablespoon to 1 avocado) and pack in small containers.
To serve
(a) Thaw $2\frac{1}{2}$ to 3 hours at room temperature and use at once. (b) Season pulp with onion, garlic or herbs.
High Quality Storage Life 2 months

Bananas
Preparation
Mash with sugar and lemon juice (8 oz/225 g sugar to 3 tablespoons lemon juice to 3 breakfastcups banana pulp). Pack in small containers.
To serve
Thaw 6 hours in unopened container in refrigerator. Use in sandwiches or cakes.

Blackberries
Preparation
Wash dark ripe berries and dry well. (a) Fast-freeze unsweetened berries on trays and pack in bags. (b) Dry sugar pack (8 oz/225 g sugar to 2 lb/1 kg fruit). (c) Sweetened purée (raw or cooked fruit).
To serve
Thaw 3 hours at room temperature. Use raw, cooked or in pies and puddings.
High Quality Storage Life 12 months

Blueberries
Preparation
Wash in chilled water and drain thoroughly. Crush fruit slightly as skins toughen on freezing. (a) Fast-freeze unsweetened berries on trays and pack in bags. (b) Dry sugar pack (4 oz/100 g sugar to 4 breakfastcups crushed berries). (c) 50% syrup pack.
To serve
Use raw, cooked or in pies and puddings.
High Quality Storage Life 12 months

Cherries

Preparation

Put in chilled water for 1 hour; remove stones. Pack in glass or plastic containers, as cherry juice remains liquid and leaks through waxed containers. (a) Dry sugar pack (8 oz/225 g sugar to 2 lb/1 kg stoned cherries). (b) 40% syrup pack for sweet cherries. (c) 50% or 60% syrup pack for sour cherries.

To serve

Thaw 3 hours at room temperature. Serve cold, or use for pies.

High Quality Storage Life   12 months

Coconut

Preparation

Grate or shred, moisten with coconut milk, and pack into bags or boxes; 4 oz/100 g sugar to 4 breakfast-cups shredded coconut may be added if liked.

To serve

Thaw 2 hours at room temperature. Drain off milk. Use for fruit salads, icings or curries.

High Quality Storage Life   2 months

Cranberries

Preparation

Wash firm glossy berries and drain. (a) Dry unsweetened pack. (b) Sweetened purée.

To serve

Cook in water and sugar while still frozen. Can be thawed $3\frac{1}{2}$ hours at room temperature.

High Quality Storage Life   12 months

Currants, Black, Red and White

Preparation

Prepare black, red or white currants by the same methods. Strip fruit from stems with a fork, wash in chilled water and dry gently. Currants can be fast-frozen on trays and the stalks stripped off before packing. This makes the job easier. (a) Dry unsweetened pack. (b) Dry sugar pack (8 oz/225 g sugar to 1 lb/450 g currants). (c) 40% syrup pack. (d) Sweetened purée (particularly blackcurrants).

To serve

(a) Thaw 45 minutes at room temperature. Use for jam, pies and puddings. (c) and (d) Use as sauce, or for drinks, ices or puddings.

High Quality Storage Life   12 months

Cranberries

Redcurrants

Damsons

Gooseberries

Damsons

Preparation

Wash in chilled water; cut in half and remove stones. (a) 50% syrup pack. (b) Sweetened purée.

To serve

Thaw at room temperature for $2\frac{1}{2}$ hours. Use cold, or for pies or puddings.

High Quality Storage Life   12 months

Dates

Preparation

(a) Wrap block dates in foil or polythene bags. (b) Remove stones from dessert dates; pack in bags or boxes.

To serve

Thaw 30 minutes at room temperature. Serve as dessert, or use for cakes or puddings.

High Quality Storage Life   12 months

Figs

Preparation

Wash fresh sweet ripe figs in chilled water; remove stems. Do not bruise. (a) Peeled or unpeeled in dry unsweetened pack. (b) 30% syrup pack for peeled figs. (c) Wrap dried dessert figs in foil or polythene bags.

To serve

Thaw $1\frac{1}{2}$ hours at room temperature. Eat raw or cooked in syrup.

High Quality Storage Life   12 months

Gooseberries

Preparation

Wash in chilled water and dry. For pies, freeze fully ripe fruit; for jam, fruit may be slightly under-ripe. (a) Dry unsweetened pack. (b) 40% syrup pack. (c) Sweetened purée.

To serve

(a) and (b) Thaw $2\frac{1}{2}$ hours at room temperature. Fruit may be put into pies or cooked while still frozen. (c) Thaw $2\frac{1}{2}$ hours at room temperature and use for fools, mousses or ices.

High Quality Storage Life   12 months

Grapefruit

Preparation

Peel; remove pith; cut into segments. (a) Dry sugar pack (8 oz/225 g sugar to 2 breakfastcups segments). (b) 50% syrup pack.

To serve

Thaw $2\frac{1}{2}$ hours at room temperature.

High Quality Storage Life   12 months

Grapes

Preparation

Pack seedless varieties whole. Skin, seed other types. Pack in 30% syrup.

To serve

Thaw $2\frac{1}{2}$ hours at room temperature.

High Quality Storage Life   12 months

Greengages

Preparation

Wash in chilled water and dry. Cut in half and remove stones. Pack in 40% syrup.

To serve

Thaw $2\frac{1}{2}$ hours at room temperature.

High Quality Storage Life   12 months

Grapefruit

Kumquats
Preparation
(a) Wrap whole fruit in foil. (b) 50% syrup pack.
To serve
Thaw 2 hours at room temperature.
High Quality Storage Life (a) 2 months, (b) 12 months.

Lemons and Limes
Preparation
Peel fruit, cut in slices, and pack in 20% syrup.
To serve
Thaw 1 hour at room temperature.
High Quality Storage Life 12 months

Loganberries
Preparation
Wash berries and dry well. (a) Fast-freeze un-sweetened berries on trays and pack in bags. (b) Dry sugar pack (8 oz/225 g sugar to 2 lb/1 kg fruit). (c) 50% syrup pack. (d) Sweetened purée (cooked fruit).
To serve
Thaw 3 hours at room temperature. Use particularly for ices and mousses.
High Quality Storage Life 12 months

Grapes

Guavas
Preparation
(a) Wash fruit, cook in a little water, and purée. Pineapple juice gives better flavour than water. (b) Peel, halve and cook until tender, then pack in 30% syrup.
To serve
Thaw 1½ hours at room temperature.
High Quality Storage Life 12 months

Mangoes

Preparation

Peel ripe fruit, and pack in slices in 50% syrup. Add 1 tablespoon lemon juice to 2 pints/1 litre syrup.

To serve

Thaw 1½ hours at room temperature.

High Quality Storage Life   12 months

Melons

Preparation

Cut into cubes or balls. Toss in lemon juice and pack in 30% syrup.

To serve

Thaw unopened in refrigerator. Serve while still frosty.

High Quality Storage Life   12 months

Nectarines

Preparation

Wipe fruit, and peel or not as desired. Cut in halves or slices and brush with lemon juice. (a) 40% syrup pack. (b) Sweetened purée (fresh fruit) with 1 table-spoonful lemon juice to each 1 lb/450 g fruit.

To serve

Thaw 3 hours in refrigerator.

High Quality Storage Life   12 months

Oranges

Preparation

Peel and divide into sections or cut into slices. (a) Dry sugar pack (8 oz/225 g sugar to 3 breakfast-cups sections or slices). (b) 30% syrup. (c) Pack slices in slightly sweetened fresh orange juice.

To serve

Thaw 2½ hours at room temperature.

High Quality Storage Life   12 months

Navel oranges become bitter in the freezer. Seville oranges may be frozen whole in their skins in polythene bags for marmalade.

Peaches

Preparation

Work quickly as fruit discolours. Peel, cut in halves or slices and brush with lemon juice. (a) 40% syrup pack. (b) Sweetened purée (fresh fruit) with 1 table-spoon lemon juice to each 1 lb/450 g fruit.

To serve

Thaw 3 hours in refrigerator.

High Quality Storage Life   12 months

Pears

Preparation

Pears should be ripe, but not over-ripe. They dis-colour quickly and do not retain their delicate flavour in the freezer. Peel and quarter fruit, remove cores, and dip pieces in lemon juice. Poach in 30% syrup for 1½ minutes. Drain and cool. Pack in cold 30% syrup.

To serve

Thaw 3 hours at room temperature.

High Quality Storage Life   12 months

Peaches

Mandarin Oranges

44

Persimmons
Preparation
(a) Wrap whole fruit in foil. (b) Peel and freeze in 50% syrup adding 1 dessertspoon lemon juice to 2 pints/1 litre syrup. (c) Sweetened purée (fresh fruit).
To serve
Thaw 3 hours at room temperature. Use unpeeled raw fruit as soon as it has thawed or it will darken.
High Quality Storage Life (a) 2 months, (b) 12 months

Pineapple
Preparation
Use fully-ripe fruit. Peel and cut into slices or chunks. (a) Dry unsweetened pack, separated by cellophane. (b) Dry sugar pack (4 oz/100 g sugar to 1 lb/450 g fruit). (c) 30% syrup pack. (d) Crush fruit and mix 4 oz/100 g sugar to 2 cups fruit.
To serve
Thaw 3 hours at room temperature.
High Quality Storage Life 12 months

Plums
Preparation
Wash in chilled water and dry. Cut in half and remove stones. Pack in 40% syrup.
To serve
Thaw 2½ hours at room temperature.
High Quality Storage Life 12 months

Plums

Pomegranates
Preparation
(a) Cut ripe fruit in half; scoop out juice sacs and pack in 50% syrup. (b) Extract juice and sweeten to taste. Freeze in ice cube trays, and wrap frozen cubes in foil for storage.
To serve
Thaw 3 hours at room temperature.
High Quality Storage Life 12 months

Quinces
Preparation
Peel core and slice. Simmer in boiling 20% syrup for 20 minutes. Cool and pack in cold 20% syrup.
To serve
Thaw 3 hours at room temperature.
High Quality Storage Life 12 months

Raspberries
Preparation
(a) Dry unsweetened pack. (b) Dry sugar pack (4 oz/100 g sugar to 1 lb/450 g fruit). (c) 30% syrup. (d) Sweetened purée (fresh fruit).
To serve
Thaw 3 hours at room temperature.
High Quality Storage Life 12 months

Rhubarb

Preparation

Wash sticks in cold running water, and trim to required length. (a) Blanch sticks 1 minute, then wrap in foil or polythene. (b) 40% syrup pack. (c) Sweetened purée (cooked fruit).

To serve

Thaw 3 hours at room temperature. Raw fruit can be cooked while still frozen.

High Quality Storage Life   12 months

Strawberries

Preparation

Use ripe, mature and firm fruit. Pick over fruit, removing hulls. (a) Grade for size in dry unsweetened pack. (b) Dry sugar pack (4 oz/100 g sugar to 1 lb/450 g fruit). Fruit may be sliced or lightly crushed. (c) 40% syrup for whole or sliced fruit. (d) Sweetened purée (fresh fruit).

To serve

Thaw 1½ hours at room temperature.

High Quality Storage Life   12 months

Strawberries are delicious with ice cream and whipped cream.

Freezing Meat

Both raw and cooked meat usually store extremely well in the freezer. But it is important to choose high-quality raw meat for storage, whether fresh or frozen, since freezing does not improve poor meat in either texture or flavour (although tender meat may become a little more tender in storage).

Many authorities feel that fresh meat should not be frozen in domestic freezers, since it is not possible to achieve the very low temperatures thought necessary for successful freezing. This point should be thought about carefully when buying in bulk for the freezer. It is also important not to overload the freezer with bulky quantities of meat at the expense of other items, and to keep a good regular turnover of supplies. One good compromise is to use the freezer for keeping special high quality cuts, or those which are not often obtainable, such as pork

fillet, veal and fillet steak, together with a variety of prepared dishes made from the cheaper cuts which are useful when time is likely to be short for food preparation. Fresh meat must be hung for the required time before freezing.

Choosing Meat for the Freezer
Meat should be chosen with the family needs in mind. The better cuts are bound to be more popular, but bulk buying will be a false economy if the family does not eat the cheaper cuts at all. Meat must be of good quality whatever the cut, and must be properly hung (beef 8–12 days; lamb 5–7 days; pork and veal chilled only). Before buying bulk meat, check the diagrams given and suggested uses for each part of the animal, and see if this will fit into the family eating plan.

Beef

THE BETTER CUTS	SUGGESTED USES
Sirloin	Roasting, preferably on the bone Grilling as Sirloin Steak 　Entrecôte Steak 　Porterhouse Steak 　T-bone Steak
Fillet	Roasting in pastry case Grilling as Châteaubriand 　Fillet Steak 　Tournedos (trimmed)

THE BETTER CUTS	SUGGESTED USES
Rump Steak	Roasting in the piece Grilling
Fore Ribs, Wing Ribs, Back Ribs	Roasting preferably on the bone
Top Ribs	Grilling as Minute Steak (thin)
Topside	Roasting, if larded Pot Roasting

THE ECONOMY CUTS	
Top Rump or Thick Flank	Pot Roasting
Flank	Pot Roasting (if boned and rolled)

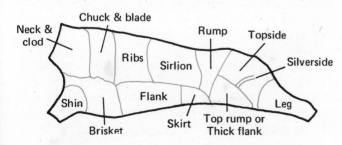

Brisket	Slow Roasting (if de-fatted and rolled)
	Pot Roasting
Silverside	Pot Roasting
Shin	Stewing
	Stock
Leg	Stewing
	Stock
Neck and Clod	Stewing
	Stock
Chuck and Blade	Stewing
	Pies and Puddings
Skirt	Stewing
	Pies and Puddings

Lamb and Mutton

THE BETTER CUTS	SUGGESTED USES
Saddle (Double Loin)	Roasting
Loin	Roasting (on or off bone)
	Chops
Leg (Fillet End and Knuckle End)	Roasting
	Boiling
Shoulder (Blade End and Knuckle End)	Roasting (on or off bone)

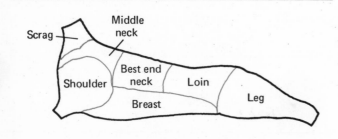

THE ECONOMY CUTS

Best End of Neck	Roasting (chined, and as Crown of Lamb)
	Cutlets
	Stewing
Middle Neck	Stewing

Scrag End of Neck	Stewing
Breast of Lamb	Roasting (boned, stuffed and rolled)
	Stewing

Pork

THE BETTER CUTS	SUGGESTED CUTS
Leg	Roasting (on or off bone)
Loin	Roasting (on or off bone)

THE ECONOMY CUTS	
Blade	Roasting
Spare Rib	Roasting
Hand and Spring	Roasting (boned, stuffed and rolled)
Belly	Roasting (boned)
	Grilling (slices)
	Pâté

Preparation for Freezing Meat

Bulk supplies of meat should be packaged in quantities which can be used up on a single occasion if possible. Ideally, meat should be boned and the surplus fat removed so as not to take up unnecessary freezer space; if the bones are *not* removed, the ends should be wrapped in several layers of greaseproof paper to avoid piercing freezer wrappings. Meat must be carefully labelled for identification, as identification may be difficult otherwise. Air must be excluded from the packages so that the freezer wrap can touch the surface of the meat all over.

If a whole animal or a variety of different meats are being prepared for freezing at one time, the offal should be processed first, then pork, veal and lamb, and finally beef as this will keep best under refrigeration if delays occur. Normally, not more

Roast beef fillet is best served in thick slices with a selection of vegetables and potato croquettes.

than 4 lb/2 kg of meat per cubic foot of freezer space should be frozen at one time for good results.

The wrapping for meat must be strong, since oxygen from the air which may penetrate wrappings affects fat and may cause rancidity (pork is the most subject to this problem). In addition to moisture-vapour-proof wrapping, an overwrap of brown paper, greaseproof paper or stockinette will protect packages and will guard against punctures from projecting bones or other packets; place the label on the outside of this wrapping. It is worth taking this precaution, since meat is likely to be the most costly item stored in the freezer.

Cooking Frozen Meat

Frozen meat can be cooked when thawed or un-thawed, but partial or complete thawing helps it to retain its juiciness. Thin cuts of meat and minced meat may toughen if cooked while still frozen. Offal must always be completely thawed. All meat should be thawed in its wrapping, and preferably in a refrigerator since slow thawing is required. Allow 5 hours per lb/450 g in a refrigerator and 2 hours per lb/450 g at room temperature. If it is really necessary to hurry thawing, this can be done in a cool oven (200°F/100°C/Gas Mark $\frac{1}{4}$ allowing 25 minutes per lb/450 g but the meat's flavour will not be so good. If meat must be cooked from the frozen state, un-

Kebabs can be quickly assembled from food in the freezer and may be grilled or cooked on the barbecue.

thawed large cuts will take 1½ times as long as fresh ones; smaller thin cuts will take 1¼ times as long. When thawing offal, sausages and mince, allow 1½ hours at room temperature or 3 hours in a refrigerator for 1 lb/450 g meat.

Frozen meat can be roasted, braised, grilled, fried or stewed in the same way as fresh meat. In any roasting process, however, it is best to use a slow oven method (for beef, use 300°F/150°C/Gas Mark 2, and also for lamb; for pork use 350°F/180°C/Gas Mark 4. Chops and steaks will cook while still frozen if put into a thick frying pan just rubbed with fat and cooked very gently for the first 5 minutes on each side, then browned more quickly. Meat should be cooked as soon as it is thawed, and still cold, to prevent loss of juices.

Here are notes on preparing, packing, storing and cooking various kinds of meat:

Casseroles and Stews

Preparation

Use a standard recipe, but slightly undercook vegetables. Do not add potatoes, rice or pasta. Cool completely and remove surplus fat. Pack in boxes or in foil-lined casserole, making sure meat is covered with liquid. When frozen, remove foil package from casserole for storage.

To serve

Heat in double boiler or in oven at 350°F/180°C/Gas Mark 4 for 45 minutes.

High Quality Storage Life　2 months

Cubed Meat

Preparation

Package in usable quantities. Trim fat and cut meat into neat pieces. Press tightly into bags or boxes, removing air.

Casseroles are a useful dish for bulk cooking.

To serve
Thaw in wrappings in refrigerator for 3 hours (1½ hours at room temperature).
High Quality Storage Life   2 months

Ham
Preparation
Package in the piece rather than sliced. Pack in freezer paper, foil or polythene, and overwrap. Vacuum-packed bacon may be frozen in its packing. Storage life is limited as salt causes rancidity.
To serve
Thaw in wrappings in refrigerator.
High Quality Storage Life 3 months (whole); 1 month (sliced)

Hearts, Kidneys, Sweetbreads, Tongue
Preparation
Wash and dry thoroughly. Remove blood vessels and pipes. Wrap in cellophane or polythene and pack in bags or boxes. Off-flavours may develop if offal is not packed with care.
To serve
Thaw in wrappings in refrigerator for 3 hours (1½ hours at room temperature).
High Quality Storage Life   2 months

Joints
Preparation
Trim surplus fat. Bone and roll if possible. Pad sharp bones. Wipe meat. Pack in polythene bag or sheeting, freezer paper or foil. Remove air. Freeze quickly.
To serve
Thaw in wrappings in refrigerator, allow 5 hours per lb/450 g. Roast by slow-oven method (300°F/150°C/Gas Mark 2 for beef and lamb; 350°F/180°C/Gas Mark 4 for pork).
High Quality Storage Life Beef 12 months; Lamb 9 months; Pork 6 months; Veal 9 months.

Liver
Preparation
Package whole or in slices. Separate slices with greaseproof paper or cellophane.
To serve
Thaw in wrappings in refrigerator for 3 hours (1½ hours at room temperature).
High Quality Storage Life   2 months

Meat (Cooked)
Preparation
Avoid freezing whole cooked joints, steaks or chops, and fried meats, which tend to toughness, dryness and rancidity when frozen. (a) Slice cooked meat in ¼ in/6 mm slices and separate with greaseproof paper or cellophane. Pack tightly in boxes or foil dishes with lids. (b) Slice meat and pack in gravy or sauce, thickened with cornflour. Pack in foil dishes with lids.
To serve
(a) Thaw in wrappings in refrigerator for 3 hours. Separate slices and dry on absorbent paper. (b) Heat in container at 350°F/180°C/Gas Mark 4 for 30 minutes.
High Quality Storage Life   2 months

Meat Pies
Preparation
(a) Prepare and cook pie in foil container. Before filling, brush bottom crust with melted fat to prevent sogginess. Cool and wrap in foil or in polythene bag. (b) Prepare and cook meat filling. Put into foil container and cover with fresh pastry. Wrap in foil or in polythene bag.
To serve
(a) Thaw in refrigerator for 6 hours to serve cold. Heat at 375°F/190°C/Gas Mark 5 for 1 hour to serve hot. (b) Remove wrappings. Bake at 400°F/200°C/Gas Mark 6 for 1 hour.
High Quality Storage Life   2 months

Sausages are always a useful freezer item, and need not be thawed before cooking.

Minced Meat
Preparation
(a) Use good quality mince without fat. Pack in bags or boxes. Do not add salt. Remove air. Freeze quickly. (b) Shape mince into patties, separated, and pack in bags or boxes. Remove air. Freeze quickly.
To serve
Thaw in wrappings in refrigerator for 3 hours (1½ hours at room temperature). Can be used while frozen, but may be tough.
High Quality Storage Life   2 months

Sausages and Sausage Meat
Preparation
Omit salt in preparation. Pack in usable quantities. Wrap tightly in freezer paper, foil or polythene.
To serve
Thaw in wrappings in refrigerator for 2 hours. Sausages can be cooked while frozen.
High Quality Storage Life   1 month

Steaks and Chops
Preparation
Package in usable quantities. Separate pieces of meat with greaseproof paper or Clingfilm. Pack in polythene bag or sheeting, freezer paper or foil. Remove air. Freeze quickly.
To serve
Thaw in wrappings in refrigerator or use while frozen. Cook gently on both sides in a lightly-oiled thick pan. Brown to serve.
High Quality Storage Life   6–12 months (according to type of meat)

Tripe
Preparation
Cut in 1 in/2·5 cm squares and pack tightly in bags or boxes.
To serve
Thaw in wrappings in refrigerator for 3 hours (1½ hours at room temperature).
High Quality Storage Life   2 months

Meat Pudding
Preparation
(a) Prepare pudding with suet crust to standard recipe. Cook in foil or polythene basin and cool quickly. Wrap tightly in foil. (b) Cook meat filling and pack in foil or polythene basins for freezing.
To serve
Remove wrapping. Cover pastry with foil and cook frozen pudding for 3 hours. (b) Remove lids. Cover with fresh suet pastry, cook 3 hours.
High Quality Storage Life   2 months

Shepherd's Pie
Preparation
Make from fresh or cooked meat, using plenty of stock or gravy to keep moist. Cool meat completely and put into foil container. Prepare mashed potatoes and cool completely. Spread on meat. Cover with foil or pack in polythene bag for freezing.
To serve
Bake at 400°F/200°C/Gas Mark 6 for 45 minutes until potatoes are golden.
High Quality Storage Life   2 months

Freezing Bacon

Buying Bacon for Freezing
(a) Freshness of the bacon is the first vital step to successful freezing. Try and get the bacon the day that the retailer gets delivery from his supplier.
(b) Determine storage period in relation to freshness, and reduce the recommended period if in doubt.
(c) Smoked bacon can be stored for longer than unsmoked bacon.
(d) The quicker bacon is frozen right through, the better it will be. It is therefore inadvisable to freeze pieces weighing more than 5 lb/2·5 kg.

Preparing Bacon for Freezing
(a) **Freshly cut bacon joints.** (i) Determine the size of joint to be required for each meal and cut to this size; (ii) wrap each piece in foil, allowing ample covering; (iii) exclude as much air as possible; (iv) place each parcel of bacon into a polythene bag. The thicker the bag the better; (v) again exclude as much air as possible. Clip or tie the bag immediately; (vi) mark date and content on each packet.
(b) **Bacon rashers, chops and steaks.** It may be necessary to freeze these small pieces of bacon but storage time is much less than for joints, only 2 to 4 weeks. This is because so much of the meat and fat surface has been exposed to air with risk of rancidity developing. It is more practical to buy vacuum packed bacon which can be stored in a refrigerator for the same periods. ½ lb/225 g packets which can be thawed and eaten promptly are recommended. If freezing, say, before going away on holiday, follow packing instructions for bacon joints.

Freezing Vacuum Packed Bacon
Vacuum packing of bacon is the ideal preparation for storage in the freezer because air has already been withdrawn from the packet. Vacuum packing is a commercial process and cannot be undertaken at home. Vacuum packed rashers and joints are almost always available in all shops.

A lot of vacuum packed bacon is so marked; but as vacuum-packing can be confused with other types of wrappings, it is advisable to check this if one is in doubt.

To prepare these packets for the freezer, inspect each one to ensure the vacuum is not damaged, i.e. the bacon should not be loose in the packet. Wrap the packets in foil, and label.

Thawing Frozen Bacon
(a) **Joints.** Allow bacon plenty of time to thaw slowly, preferably in a refrigerator. Bacon can be thawed at room temperature before cooking. Time required depends on the thickness of the piece and the temperature. The wrapping should be removed as soon as possible during thawing.
(b) **Bacon rashers and small pieces** may be thawed overnight in the refrigerator or dipped in hot water for a few minutes until soft. Dry on kitchen paper before cooking.
(c) **Vacuum packed joints.** These should be thawed in the bag, in the refrigerator or at room temperature. Cook immediately following instructions on packet. Note: If time is short, joints may be thawed in running water, but should be wrapped in a plastic bag to prevent them getting wet.

Cooking Frozen Bacon
All frozen bacon should be cooked immediately it has thawed. The usual cooking methods – boiling, grilling, frying and baking – are suitable. Once cooked, the bacon will keep 1–2 days in a refrigerator.
Do not re-freeze after thawing either in the raw or cooked state.
Cooked fresh bacon joints should not be frozen as this may result in poor appearance with keeping and flavour problems. Small pieces can be used for flavouring stews or such dishes as Quiche Lorraine which are to be put in the freezer for short periods. The dishes should be well wrapped before freezing.

Bacon can be bulk-purchased and is always welcome for a traditional English breakfast.

Leftover Bacon

Preparation

Crumble cooked bacon and freeze in small containers.

To serve

Add to casseroles or use on potatoes, cheese or fish dishes. Thaw in refrigerator for 2 hours to use in sandwich spreads.

High Quality Storage Life   2 weeks

High Quality Storage Life

1. Bacon joints wrapped as recommended:
   (a) Smoked bacon up to 8 weeks
   (b) Unsmoked bacon up to 5 weeks
2. Vacuum packed bacon joints up to 10 weeks.
3. Vacuum packed rashers or steaks up to 10 weeks.
4. Foil-wrapped rashers, chops or steaks, smoked, 2–4 weeks only.

Freezing Poultry and Game

Preparation for Freezing Poultry

Birds to be frozen should be in perfect condition. They should be starved for 24 hours before killing, then hung and bled well. When the bird is plucked, it is important to avoid skin damage; if scalding, beware of over-scalding which may increase the chance of freezer-burn (grey spots occurring during storage). The bird should be cooled in a refrigerator or cold larder for 12 hours, drawn and completely cleaned. With geese and ducks, it is particularly important to see the oil glands are removed as these will cause tainting.

Packing

A whole bird should be carefully trussed to make a neat shape for packing. Birds can be frozen as halves or joints. When packing pieces, it is not always ideal to pack a complete bird in each package; it may be more useful ultimately if all drumsticks are packaged together, all breasts or all wings, according to the way in which the flesh will be cooked.

Giblets have only a storage life of 2 months, so unless a whole bird is to be used within that time, it is not advisable to pack them inside the bird. Giblets should be cleaned, washed, dried and chilled, then wrapped in moisture-vapour-proof paper or a bag, excluding air; frozen in batches, they can be used for soups, stews or pies. Livers should be treated in the same way, and packaged in batches for use in omelettes, risotto or pâtés.

Bones of poultry joints should be padded with paper or foil to avoid tearing the freezer wrappings. Joints should be divided by two layers of cellophane. Bones of young birds may turn brown in storage, but this does not affect flavour or quality.

Stuffings

Stuffing can, if necessary, be put into a bird before freezing, but it is not advisable as the storage life of stuffing is only about 1 month. Pork sausage stuffing should not be used; if a bird must be stuffed, a breadcrumb stuffing is best. It is better to package stuffing separately if some is available when the bird is put into freezer storage; otherwise, it is not worth making specially, as it can easily be prepared while the bird is thawing.

Cooked Poultry

Old birds such as boiling fowls are best frozen after being cooked; the meat should be stripped from the bones, and frozen; or it can be made at once into pies or casseroles, while the carcass is simmered in the cooking liquid to make strong stock for freezing. Slices of cooked poultry can be frozen on their own, or in sauce (the latter method is preferable to

Chicken joints make particularly useful freezer items.

prevent drying out). If the meat is frozen without sauce, slices should be divided by two sheets of cellophane and then closely packed together excluding air. Roast and fried poultry frozen to be eaten cold are not particularly successful; on thawing they tend to exude moisture and become flabby.

Thawing
Uncooked poultry must thaw completely before cooking. Thawing in the refrigerator will allow slow, even thawing; thawing at room temperature will be twice as fast but the product will be much less satisfactory. A 4–5 lb/2–2·5 kg chicken will thaw overnight in a refrigerator and will take 6 hours at room temperature. A turkey weighing 9 lb/4·5 kg will take 36 hours; as much as 3 days should be allowed for a very large bird. A thawed bird can be stored for up to 24 hours in a refrigerator, but no more.

All poultry should be thawed in the unopened freezer wrappings.

Preparation for Freezing Game
Freeze raw birds or animals which are young and well shot. Roast game is usefully frozen in its season, to eat cold later; but on thawing it exudes moisture so that the flesh may be flabby. Old or badly shot game is usually best converted immediately into made-up dishes such as casseroles.

All game intended for freezing should be hung to its required state *before* freezing, as hanging after thawing will result in the flesh going bad. Grouse, pheasant and partridge should be plucked and drawn before freezing. So should any waterfowl fed on fish. Plover, quail, snipe and woodcock should be plucked but not drawn. Hare and rabbit are handled like poultry. Venison is treated like beef; it is best if aged for 5 to 6 days before freezing if the carcass is in good condition and should be chilled soon after shooting, in a cold larder.

All game should be kept cool between shooting and freezing; care should be taken to remove as much shot as possible, and to make sure the shot wounds are thoroughly clean. Birds should be bled as soon as shot, and then hung to individual taste. After plucking and drawing, the cavity should be thoroughly washed and drained and the body wiped with a damp cloth. The birds should then be packed, cooled and frozen like poultry.

Thawing Game
All game should be thawed in its sealed freezer package; thawing in a refrigerator is more uniform, but of course takes longer. In a refrigerator, allow 5 hours per lb/450 g thawing time; at room temper-

ature, allow 2 hours per lb/450 g. Start cooking as soon as game is thawed and still cold, to prevent loss of juices.

Chicken
Preparation
Hang and cool. Pluck and draw and pack giblets separately. Truss whole bird or cut in joints. Chill 12 hours. Pack in bag, removing air.
To serve
Thaw in bag in refrigerator. Allow 4–5 lb/2–2·5 kg bird to thaw overnight (6 hours at room temperature).
High Quality Storage Life 12 months

Duck
Preparation
Hang and cool. Remove oil glands. Pluck and draw and pack giblets separately. Chill 12 hours. Pack in bag, removing air.
To serve
Thaw in bag in refrigerator. Allow 4–5 lb/2–2·5 kg bird to thaw overnight (6 hours at room temperature).
High Quality Storage Life 6 months

Giblets
Preparation
(a) Clean, wash, dry and chill. Pack in bag, removing

Roast chicken.

Roast goose is delicious served with slices of orange.

air. (b) Cook and pack in cooking liquid in box.
To serve
(a) Thaw in bag in refrigerator for 2 hours. (b) Heat gently and use for soups, stews or pies.
High Quality Storage Life (a) 2 months, (b) 1 month

Goose
Preparation
Hang and cool. Remove oil glands. Pluck and draw and pack giblets separately. Chill 12 hours. Pack in bag, removing air.
To serve
Thaw in bag in refrigerator. Allow small bird to thaw overnight; large bird will need 24 hours.
High Quality Storage Life 6 months

Guinea Fowl
Preparation
Hang and cool. Pluck and draw and pack giblets separately. Truss and chill 12 hours. Pack in bag, removing air.
To serve
Thaw in bag in refrigerator for 8 hours. As this is a dry bird, lard before roasting.
High Quality Storage Life 12 months

Grouse (12 August–10 December) Partridge (1 September–1 February) Pheasant (1 October–1 February)
Preparation
Remove shot and clean wounds. Bleed as soon as shot, keep cool and hang to taste. Pluck, draw and truss. Pad bones. Pack in bag, removing air. If birds are old or badly shot, prepare as casseroles, soups, pies.
To serve
Thaw in bag in refrigerator for 5 hours per lb/450 g (2 hours per lb/450 g at room temperature). Cook as soon as thawed.
High Quality Storage Life 6 months

Hare makes an interesting and unusual casserole dish.

Livers
Preparation
Clean, wash, dry and chill. Pack in bag, removing air.
To serve
Thaw in bag in refrigerator for 2 hours.
High Quality Storage Life 2 months

Pigeons
Preparation
Remove shot and clean wounds. Prepare and pack as feathered game. Pigeons are usefully prepared as casseroles or pies for freezing.
To serve
Thaw in bag in refrigerator for 5 hours per lb/450 g (2 hours per lb/450 g at room temperature).
High Quality Storage Life 6 months

Plover, Quail, Snipe, Woodcock
Preparation
Remove shot and clean wounds. Prepare as other feathered game but do not draw. Pad bones. Pack in bag, removing air.
To serve
Thaw in bag in refrigerator for 5 hours per lb/450 g (2 hours per lb/450 g at room temperature). Cook as soon as thawed.
High Quality Storage Life 6 months

Rabbits and Hares
Preparation
Clean shot wounds. Behead and bleed as soon as possible, collecting hare's blood if needed for cooking. Hang for 24 hours in a cool place. Skin, clean and wipe. Cut into joints and wrap each piece in cellophane. Pack in usable quantities in bags. Pack blood in box.
To serve
Thaw in bag in refrigerator for 5 hours per lb/450 g (2 hours per lb/450 g at room temperature).
High Quality Storage Life 6 months

Stuffing
Preparation
(a) Prepare stuffing to standard recipe. Pack in box or bag. (b) Prepare stuffing and form into balls. Deep-fry, cool and pack into box or bag.
To serve
(a) Thaw in bag in refrigerator for 2 hours. (b) Thaw in bag in refrigerator for 2 hours. Put into roasting tin or casserole 10 minutes before serving.
High Quality Storage Life 1 month

Roast turkey makes a festive dish throughout the year.

Turkey
Preparation
Hang and cool. Pluck and draw, and pack giblets separately. Truss whole or cut in joints. Chill for 12 hours. Pack in bag, removing air.
To serve
Thaw in bag in refrigerator for 2 days (small birds); 3 days (large birds).
High Quality Storage Life   12 months

Venison
Preparation
Clean shot wounds. Keep the carcass cold until butchered. Behead, bleed, skin and clean, wash and wipe flesh. Hang in a cool place for 5 days. Joint and pack in bags, removing air. Freeze the good joints, but prepare other cuts as cooked dishes for freezing.
To serve
Thaw in wrappings in refrigerator for 4 hours. Remove from wrappings and put into marinade. Continue thawing, allowing 5 hours per lb/450 g. Lard meat for roasting. Use the marinade for gravy or casseroles. For the marinade, which will prevent the meat from being dry when cooked, mix $\frac{1}{2}$ pint/ 250 ml red wine, $\frac{1}{2}$ pint/250 ml vinegar, 1 large sliced onion, parsley, thyme and bayleaf. Turn the venison frequently while marinating.
High Quality Storage Life 8 months

Freezing Fish and Shellfish

Only really fresh fish can be frozen, since it must be processed within 24 hours. Therefore it is not advisable to freeze shop-purchased fish.

Cooked fish can be frozen in sauces or pies, or ready-fried, but it is rarely worth the trouble to cook fish specially for freezing. Fish should never be overcooked and the time taken to reheat will not only spoil flavour and rob the fish of any nutritive value, but will also take as long as the original cooking.

Fatty fish (i.e. haddock, halibut, herring, mackerel, salmon, trout, turbot) will keep for 4 months at most. White fish (i.e. cod, plaice, sole, whiting) will keep for 6 months. Shellfish are best stored no longer than 1 month. It is wise to keep fish for only the shortest possible time in the freezer.

It is useful to freeze smoked fish such as bloaters, kippers and haddock sometimes.

Preparation for Freezing

Since the fish must be fresh, one must clean home-caught fish ready for freezing as soon as it is caught. The fish should be killed at once, scaled if necessary and fins removed. Small fish can be left whole; large fish should have heads and tails removed, or can be divided into steaks. Flat fish and herrings are best gutted, and flat fish skinned and filleted. White fish should be washed well in salted water during cleaning to remove blood and membranes, but fatty fish should be washed in fresh water.

Freezing Methods

There are four ways of preparing fish for freezing, the first two being the most common.

(a) Dry Pack. Separate pieces of fish with double thickness of cellophane, wrap in moisture-vapour-proof paper, carton or bag; seal and freeze. Be sure the paper is in close contact with the fish to exclude air which will dry the fish and make it tasteless. Freeze quickly on the floor of the freezer.

(b) Brine Pack. (This is *not* suitable for fatty fish, as salt tends to oxidise and lead to rancidity). Dip fish into cold salted water (1 tablespoon salt to 2 pints/1 litre water), drain, wrap and seal. Do not keep brine-dipped fish longer than 3 months.

(c) Acid Pack. Citric acid preserves the colour and flavour of fish; ascorbic acid is an anti-oxidant which stops the development of rancidity in fish which can cause off-flavours and smells. A chemist can provide an ascorbic-citric acid powder, to be diluted in a proportion of 1 part powder to 100 parts of water. Dip fish into this solution, drain, wrap and seal.

(d) Solid Ice Pack. Small fish, steaks or fillets can be covered with water in refrigerator trays or loaf tins and frozen into solid blocks. The fish should be separated by double paper as usual. Remove ice blocks from pan, wrap in freezer paper and store. The fish can also be frozen in a solid ice pack in large waxed tubs; cover the fish completely to within $\frac{1}{2}$ in/1·25 cm of container top and crumple a piece of Cellophane over the top of the fish before closing the lid. The only advantage in this solid ice method is a saving of containers and wrapping material.

Freezing Large Whole Fish

Sometimes a large whole fish may be wanted; if so, it can be frozen whole, but is best protected by 'glazing'. Salmon and salmon trout are obvious examples, or perhaps a haddock or halibut to serve stuffed for a party.

To Glaze a Large Fish

First clean the fish. Then place the unwrapped fish against the freezer wall in the coldest possible part of the freezer. When the fish is frozen solid, dip it very quickly into very cold water so a thin coating of ice will form. Return fish to freezer for an hour, and repeat process. Continue until ice has built up to $\frac{1}{2}$ in/1·25 cm thickness. The fish can be stored without wrappings for 2 weeks, but is better

Mackerel

Cod

wrapped in freezer paper for longer storage.

Smoked Fish
Bloaters, kippers and haddock can be wrapped and frozen and will keep for 2 months. No special preparation is necessary.

Shellfish
Freshly caught shellfish can be frozen immediately after cooking. Scallops and oysters are frozen raw. Shrimps can be frozen when cooked, or after being potted in butter.

Thawing and Cooking
All fish should be thawed slowly in unopened wrappings. A 1 lb/450 g or 1 pint/500 ml package takes about 3 hours at room temperature, or 6 hours in a refrigerator. Frozen fish may be used for boiling, steaming, grilling or frying; except for frying, complete thawing is not necessary.

Crab
Preparation
Cook, drain and cool. Clean crab and remove edible meat. Pack into boxes or bags.
To serve
Thaw in container in refrigerator. Serve cold, or add to hot dishes.
High Quality Storage Life   1 month

Salmon

Fatty Fish (Haddock, Halibut, Mackerel, Salmon, Trout, Turbot)
Preparation
Clean. Fillet or cut in steaks if liked, or leave whole. Separate pieces of fish with double thickness of Clingfilm. Wrap in freezer paper, or put in box or bag. Be sure air is excluded, or fish will be dry and tasteless. Keep pack shallow. Freeze quickly. Large fish may be prepared in solid ice pack. Do not use brine pack.
To serve
Thaw large fish in unopened container in refrigerator. Cook small pieces of fish while frozen.
High Quality Storage Life   1 month

Lobster and Crayfish
Preparation
Cook, cool and split. Remove flesh and pack into boxes or bags.
To serve
Thaw in container in refrigerator. Serve cold, or add to hot dishes.
High Quality Storage Life   1 month

Mussels
Preparation
Scrub very thoroughly and remove any fibrous matter sticking out from the shell. Put in a large saucepan and cover with a damp cloth. Put over medium heat about 3 minutes until they open. Cool in the pan. Remove from shells and pack in boxes, covering with their own juice.
To serve
Thaw in container in refrigerator and cook, using as fresh fish.
High Quality Storage Life   1 month

Oysters
Preparation
Open oysters and save liquid. Wash fish in salt water (1 teaspoon salt to 1 pint/500 ml water). Pack in boxes, covering with own liquid.
To serve
Thaw in container in refrigerator. Serve raw or cooked.
High Quality Storage Life   1 month

Crayfish

Prawns

Prawns
Preparation
Cook and cool in cooking water. Remove shells.
Pack tightly in boxes or bags.
To serve
Thaw in container in refrigerator. Serve cold, or use
for cooking.
High Quality Storage Life   1 month

Scallops
Preparation
Open shells. Wash fish in salt water (1 teaspoon salt
to 1 pint/500 ml water). Pack in boxes covering with
salt water, and leaving $\frac{1}{2}$ in/1·25 cm headspace.
To serve
Thaw in container in refrigerator. Drain and cook,
using as fresh fish.
High Quality Storage Life   1 month

Shrimps

Preparation

(a) Cook and cool in cooking water. Remove shells. Pack in boxes or bags. (b) Cook and shell shrimps. Pack in waxed boxes and cover with melted spiced butter.

To serve

(a) Thaw in container in refrigerator to eat cold. Add frozen shrimps to hot dishes. (b) Thaw in container in refrigerator.

High Quality Storage Life   1 month

Smoked Fish (Bloaters, Eel, Haddock, Kippers, Mackerel, Salmon, Sprats, Trout)

Preparation

Pack fish in layers with Clingfilm between. Keep pack shallow.

To serve

To eat cold, thaw in refrigerator. Haddock and kippers may be cooked while frozen.

High Quality Storage Life   2 months

White Fish (Cod, Plaice, Sole, Whiting)

Preparation

Clean. Fillet or cut in steaks if liked, or leave whole. Separate pieces of fish with double thickness of Cellophane. Wrap in freezer paper, or put in box or bag. Be sure air is excluded, or fish will be dry and tasteless. Keep pack shallow. Freeze quickly.

To serve

Thaw large fish in unopened container in refrigerator. Cook small pieces of fish while frozen.

High Quality Storage Life   3 months

Freezing Dairy Produce

Cheese

Dairy produce should not be allowed to take up much freezer space, but it can be useful to freeze quantities of cheap fat or eggs when available; cheese left after large parties; leftover egg yolks or whites or cracked eggs bought cheaply, or thick cream brought back from a country holiday.

Butter or Margarine
Preparation
Overwrap blocks in foil or polythene.
To serve
Thaw enough for one week's use.
High Quality Storage Life 6 months (unsalted); 3 months (salted)

Cheese
Preparation
(a) Freeze hard cheese such as Cheddar in small portions (8 oz/225 g or less). Divide slices with double Clingfilm and wrap in foil or freezer paper. (b) Freeze grated cheese in polythene bags; the pieces remain separated. (c) Freeze Camembert, Port Salut, Stilton, Danish Blue and Roquefort with careful sealing to avoid drying out and cross-contamination.
To serve
(a) Thaw in open wrappings at room temperature for 2 hours. Cut while slightly frozen to avoid crumbling. (b) Sprinkle on dishes or thaw for 1 hour before adding to sauces. (c) Thaw 1 day in refrigerator and 1 day at room temperature for full flavour.
High Quality Storage Life (a) 3 months, (b) 3 months, (c) 6 months

Cream

Preparation

Use pasteurised cream, over 40% butterfat. Freeze in cartons (1 in/2·5 cm headspace).

To serve

Thaw in container at room temperature. Beat lightly with a fork to make smooth. Note that in hot drinks, oil will rise to the surface.

High Quality Storage Life   6 months

Cream Cheese

Preparation

Best blended with heavy cream and frozen as a cocktail dip in waxed tubs or rigid plastic containers.

To serve

Thaw in container in refrigerator overnight. Blend with a fork to make smooth.

High Quality Storage Life   3 months

Eggs

Preparation

Do not freeze eggs in shell. Blend lightly with a fork. Add ½ teaspoon salt or ½ teaspoon sugar to 5 eggs. Pack in waxed or rigid plastic containers. Label with number of eggs and 'salt' or 'sugar'.

To serve

Thaw in unopened container in refrigerator. Use as fresh eggs as soon as thawed. 3 tablespoons whole egg = 1 fresh egg.

High Quality Storage Life   12 months

Egg Whites

Preparation

Freeze in waxed or rigid plastic containers or in ice-cube trays. Label with number of whites.

To serve

Thaw in refrigerator, but bring to room temperature before use. Can be whipped successfully.

High Quality Storage Life   12 months

Egg Yolks

Preparation

Mix lightly with a fork. Add ½ teaspoon salt or ½ tablespoon sugar to 6 yolks. Label with number of yolks and 'salt' or 'sugar'. Can be frozen in waxed or rigid plastic containers or in ice-cube trays. Transfer cubes to polythene bags for storage.

To serve

Thaw in refrigerator. Use alone or mix with whites.

High Quality Storage Life   12 months

Milk

Preparation

Freeze homogenised milk in cartons (1 in/2·5 cm headspace).

To serve

Thaw at room temperature and use quickly.

High Quality Storage Life   1 month

Whipped Cream

Preparation

Use 1 tablespoon sugar to 1 pint/500 ml cream.
(a) Freeze in cartons (1 in/2·5 cm headspace).
(b) Pipe in rosettes, freeze on open trays and pack in boxes.

To serve

Thaw in container at room temperature. Rosettes will thaw in 15 minutes at room temperature.

High Quality Storage Life   6 months

Ice Cream

Home-made ice cream can be stored in the freezer for 3 months. Bought ice cream is best stored no longer than 1 month. If large containers of bought ice cream are stored, and not repackaged into serving sizes before storage, they should be used sooner than this after opening. When portions have been taken out of a large container, a piece of foil over the unused portion will help to retain flavour and texture.

Home-made ice cream for the freezer is best made with pure cream and gelatine or egg yolks. For immediate use, evaporated milk may be used, but the flavour is less good (before using the unopened tin of milk should be boiled for 10 minutes, cooled and left in a refrigerator overnight). A smooth commercial product cannot be produced from a home freezer. The ingredients are different and so is the equipment which gives a smooth ice cream. Sorbétières can now be bought for freezers, however, which work on the principle of the old dasher-churn, giving a constant beating which produces a relatively smooth product.

All home-made ice cream should be frozen quickly, or it will be 'grainy'. The correct emulsifying agent will help to make a smooth product. Egg, gelatine, cream or sugar syrup will stop large ice crystals forming; gelatine gives a particularly smooth ice. Whipped egg whites give lightness. Freezing diminishes sweetness, but too much sugar will prevent freezing. The correct proportion is one part sugar to four parts liquid.

Preparation for Freezing Ice Cream

Whatever emulsifying agent is used, the preparation is similar. The mixture should be packed into trays and frozen until just solid about ½ in/1·25 cm from the edge. The mixture should then be beaten quickly in a chilled bowl, and then frozen again for

Meringues, ice cream and whipped cream are easily stored in the freezer and may be assembled quickly before a meal.

a further hour. This 'freezing and beating' technique should be repeated for up to three hours. Some freezer owners save time by packing the ice cream into storage containers and freezing after the first beating, but results are less smooth, and it is preferable to complete the ice cream before packing for storage. To remove portions of ice cream from a large container, dip a scoop into boiling water before cutting into the ice cream.

To make moulds of ice cream, press the finished ice into metal moulds (if double-sided moulds are not available, use metal jelly moulds, cover tops with foil, wrap and seal). To turn out, invert mould on plate and cover metal with cloth wrung out in hot water. Two-flavoured moulds can be made by lining mould with one flavour and filling with another (chopped fruit or nuts may be added to the inner ice cream).

Basic Ice Cream
Preparation
Prepare standard recipe and freeze in trays. When completed, pack in rigid plastic boxes, filling air space with crumpled foil or Cellophane. Seal tightly.
To serve
Scoop out into dishes. Fill remaining airspace in container with crumpled foil or cellophane.
High Quality Storage Life   3 months

Fresh Fruit Ices
Preparation
Prepare standard recipe and freeze in trays. Add pieces of fresh fruit before final freezing. Pack in rigid plastic boxes, filling air space with crumpled foil or cellophane. Seal tightly.
To serve
Scoop out into dishes. Fill remaining air space in container with crumpled foil or cellophane.
High Quality Storage Life   3 months

Moulds or Bombes
Preparation
Use double-sided moulds, jelly moulds or pudding basins. Soften ice cream slightly and line the mould. Freeze for 1 hour, then put in the next layer of ice cream. Freeze again then add another ice cream, or a filling of fruit and/or liqueur. Wrap in foil, seal and freeze.
To serve
Turn out on chilled plate, using cloth wrung out in hot water. Wrap in foil and freeze 1 hour before serving.
High Quality Storage Life   3 months

Sorbets

Preparation

(a) Pack in leakproof rigid plastic or waxed containers and seal tightly, as these water ices do not freeze completely hard during storage.

(b) Pack into clean orange or lemon skins and wrap in foil, sealing tightly.

To serve

(a) Scoop on to plates or fill fresh fruit skins.

(b) Remove foil and return to freezer for 1 hour to frost the skins.

High Quality Storage Life   3 months

Custard Ice

$\frac{3}{4}$ pint/375 ml creamy milk
1 vanilla pod
2 large egg yolks
2 oz/50 g sugar
small pinch of salt
$\frac{1}{3}$ pint/200 ml double cream

Scald milk with vanilla pod. Remove pod and pour milk on to egg yolks lightly beaten with sugar and salt. Cook mixture in a double boiler until it coats the back of a spoon. Cool and strain and stir in the cream. Pour into freezing trays and beat twice during a total freezing time of about 3 hours. Pack into containers, cover and seal, and store in freezer.

Gelatine Ice

$\frac{3}{4}$ pint/375 ml creamy milk
1 vanilla pod
2 teaspoons gelatine
3 oz/75 g sugar
pinch of salt

Heat $\frac{1}{4}$ pint/125 ml milk with vanilla pod to boiling point. Soak gelatine in 2 tablespoons cold water, then put into a bowl standing in hot water until the gelatine is syrupy. Pour warm milk on to the gelatine, stir in sugar, salt and remaining milk. Remove vanilla pod and freeze mixture, beating twice during 3 hours total freezing time. Pack into containers, cover and seal, and store in freezer. This mixture is particularly good for using with such flavourings such as chocolate or caramel.

Cream Ice

1 pint/500 ml single cream
1 vanilla pod
3 oz/75 g sugar
pinch of salt

Scald cream with vanilla pod, stir in sugar and salt, and cool. Remove vanilla pod and freeze mixture to a mush. Beat well in a chilled bowl and continue freezing (about 2 hours total freezing time). Pack into containers, cover, seal and label, and store in freezer.

Flavourings for Basic Ice Creams

Flavourings should be strong and pure (e.g. vanilla pod or sugar instead of essence; liqueurs rather than flavoured essences), as they are affected by low temperature storage. Flavourings may be varied by using one of the basic recipes and adjusting to the required flavour.

Butterscotch   Cook the sugar in the recipe with 2 tablespoons butter until well browned, then add to hot milk or cream.

Caramel   Melt half the sugar in the recipe with a moderate heat, using a heavy saucepan, and add slowly to the hot milk.

Chocolate   Melt 2 oz/50 g unsweetened cooking chocolate in 4 tablespoons hot water, stir until smooth, and add to the hot milk.

Coffee   Scald 2 tablespoons ground coffee with milk or cream and strain before adding to other ingredients.

Peppermint   Use oil of peppermint, and colour lightly green.

Praline   Make as caramel flavouring, adding 4 oz/100 g blanched, toasted and finely chopped almonds.

Egg Nog   Stir in several tablespoons rum, brandy or whisky to ice cream made with egg yolks.

Ginger   Add 2 tablespoons chopped preserved ginger and 3 tablespoons ginger syrup to basic mixture.

Maple   Use maple syrup in place of sugar, add 4 oz/100 g chopped walnuts.

Pistachio   Add 1 teaspoon almond essence and 2 oz/50 g chopped pistachio nuts, and colour lightly green.

Flavourings for Ice Creams, Mixed

Mixed flavour ice creams can be prepared by adding flavoured sauces or crushed fruit to vanilla ice cream, or by making additions to some of the basic flavours. Crushed fruit such as strawberries, raspberries or canned mandarin oranges may be beaten into vanilla ice cream before packing. Chocolate or butterscotch sauce can be swirled through vanilla ice. Chopped toasted nuts or crushed nut toffee pair with vanilla, coffee or chocolate flavours. A pinch of coffee powder may be used in chocolate ice cream, or a little melted choclate in coffee ice; one of the chocolate- or coffee-flavoured liqueurs may also be used.

Freezing Bread, Cakes, Pastry and Sandwiches

Preparation for Freezing Bread and Cakes

Small cakes, buns and rolls are most easily frozen in polythene bags; small iced cakes are better packed in boxes. Large quantities of small iced cakes can be frozen in single layers, then packed in larger boxes with Clingfilm or greaseproof paper between the layers. Bread and large cakes can both be frozen in polythene bags. While it is usually most convenient to pack cakes whole, some families may need meal-size wedges or individual pieces for lunch-boxes. These pieces can be frozen individually in bags or boxes, but it is easier to slice the whole cake in wedges before freezing, and take slices as needed without thawing the whole cake.

When making cakes for freezing, it is most important to use good ingredients. Stale flour deteriorates quickly after freezing, so it is important to use fresh flour. Butter cakes retain a good flavour, but margarine is more suitable for strongly-flavoured cakes such as chocolate, and it always gives a good, light texture. Eggs should be fresh and very well beaten, as whites and yolks freeze at different speeds and this can affect the texture of the cake. Icings for freezing are best made with butter and icing sugar; cakes should *not* be filled with boiled icing or with cream as these will crumble on thawing; so will icings made with egg whites. Fruit fillings and jams will make a cake soggy, and are best added after thawing. Flavourings must always be pure, as synthetics develop off-flavours in storage (this is particularly important with vanilla, and only pure extract or vanilla sugar made with a pod should be used). If the freezer user is not an enthusiastic bread or cake cook, there is no reason why bought cakes should not be frozen for emergencies. Buns, Dundee cakes, unfilled sponges and sponge flan cases all freeze well and are very useful, but the same limitations concerning icings and fillings will apply to bought cakes as to home-baked ones. Crumpets and muffins are seasonal delicacies which can be frozen for future use.

Uncooked Yeast Mixtures

It is possible to freeze unbaked bread and buns for up to 2 weeks, but proving after freezing takes a long time, and the final texture may be heavier. If unbaked dough is frozen, it should be allowed to prove once, and either shaped for baking or kept in bulk if storage in this form is easier. Brush the surface with a little olive oil or unsalted melted butter to prevent toughening of the crust, and add a little extra sugar to sweet mixtures.

Single loaves or a quantity of dough can be packed in freezer paper or polythene, and rolls can be packed in layers separated by Clingfilm before wrapping in freezer paper or polythene.

The dough should be thawed in a moist warm place, quickly. Speed will help to give a light-textured loaf. After thawing the dough can be shaped and proved again before baking. Shaped bread and rolls should only be proved once, in a warm place, before baking.

Biscuits

Biscuits are the exception to the rule that cooked frozen goods are better than uncooked ones. Baked biscuits do freeze very well, but they store equally well in tins, so there is no advantage in using valuable freezer space for them. The most useful and time-saving way of preparing biscuits is to freeze batches of any favourite recipe in cylinder shapes, wrapped in freezer paper, polythene or foil. Over-wrapping is advisable to avoid dents in the freezer from other packages. The dough will be all the better having been frozen, giving light crisp biscuits. To use, leave in freezer wrappings in the refrigerator for 45 minutes until just beginning to soften, then cut in slices and bake; if the dough gets too soft it will be difficult to cut. If baked biscuits are to be stored, they must be carefully packed in layers in cartons with Clingfilm or greaseproof paper between layers and with crumpled-up paper in air spaces to safeguard freshness and stop breakages.

Icings and Fillings

Cakes for storage should not be filled with cream, jam or fruit. Butter icings are best, but an iced cake must be absolutely firm before wrapping and freezing. Brief chilling in the refrigerator will achieve this in hot weather. Wrappings must be removed before thawing to allow moisture to escape and to avoid smudging the icing. If sponge or flavoured cakes are to be packed for future icing later on, the layers can be stacked with Clingfilm, foil or greaseproof paper between them, and can be separated easily for filling when thawed.

Flavourings and Decorations

Flavourings must be pure for all icings and fillings, and vanilla extract or vanilla sugar should be used when vanilla is needed. Highly spiced foods may develop off-flavours, so spice cakes should not usually be frozen, though an ordinary gingerbread is perfectly satisfactory. Chocolate, coffee, and fruit-flavoured cakes freeze very well. There is no particular advantage in decorating cakes before they are frozen, and nuts, coloured balls, grated chocolate etc. should be put on when the cake is fully thawed, just before serving; otherwise moisture may be absorbed and colour changes affect the appearance of the cake.

Preparation for Freezing Pastry

Short pastry and flaky pastry freeze equally well either cooked or uncooked, but a standard balanced recipe should be used for best results. Commercially-frozen pastry is one of the most useful and successful freezer stand-bys. Pastry can be stored unbaked or baked; baked pastry keeps longer (baked: 6 months; unbaked: 4 months), but unbaked pastry has a better flavour and scent, and is crisper and flakier.

Unbaked Pastry

Pastry can be rolled, formed into a square, wrapped in greaseproof paper, then in foil or polythene for freezing. This pastry takes time to thaw, and may crumble when rolled. It should be thawed slowly, then cooked as fresh pastry and eaten fresh-baked, *not* returned to the freezer in cooked form.

Baked Pastry

Flan cases, patty cases and vol-au-vent cases are all useful to keep ready-baked. For storage, it is best to keep them in the cases in which they are baked or in foil cases. Small cases can be packed in boxes in layers with paper between. Baked cases should be thawed in their wrappings at room temperature

before filling. They can be heated in a low oven if a hot filling is to be used.

Preparation for Freezing Pies

Frozen pies provide useful meals, and are a neat way of storing surplus fruit, meat and poultry. Large pies can be stored, also turnovers, pasties and individual fruit pies. Both pies and flans can be stored baked or unbaked. A baked pie usually keeps longer (depending on the filling), but an unbaked pie has a better flavour and scent, and the pastry is crisper and flakier. Almost all fillings can be used, except those with custard which separates. Meringue toppings should not be used as they toughen and dry during storage.

Baked Pies

Pies can be baked in the normal way, then cooled quickly before freezing. A pie is best prepared and frozen in foil, but can be stored in a rust-proof and crack-proof container. The container should be put into freezer paper or polythene for freezing. A cooked pie should be heated at 375°F/190°C/Gas Mark 5 for 40–50 minutes for a double-crust pie and for 30–50 minutes for a one-crust pie, depending on size. Cooked pies can also be thawed in their wrappings at room temperature and eaten without reheating.

Unbaked Pies

Pies can be prepared with or without a bottom crust. To prevent sogginess, it is better to freeze unbaked pies before wrapping them. Air vents should be cut in the top crust after freezing, not before. To bake pies, cut slits in the frozen top crust and bake unthawed like fresh pies, allowing about 10 minutes longer than the normal cooking time.

Fruit Fillings

If the surface of the bottom crust of fruit pies is brushed with egg white, it will not get soggy. Fruit pies can be made with cooked or uncooked fillings. Apples tend to brown if stored in a pie for more than 4 weeks, even if treated with lemon juice, so it is better to combine frozen pastry and frozen apples to make a pie.

If time is likely to be short, it is often convenient to freeze ready-made fruit pie fillings ahead, ready to fit into fresh pastry when needed; this is also a good way of freezing surplus fruit in a handy form. The mixture is best frozen in a sponge-cake tin or an oven-glass pie plate lined with foil, then removed from container and wrapped in foil for storage; the same container can then be used for making the pie later on. A little cornflour or flaked tapioca added to fruit when cooking it gives a firm pie filling which cuts well and does not seep through the pastry.

Meat Fillings

Meat pies can be completely cooked so that they need only be reheated for serving. Preparation time is saved however if the meat filling is cooked and cooled, then topped with pastry. If the pie is made in this form, the time taken to cook the pastry is enough to heat the meat filling, and the process takes only a little longer than heating the whole pie.

Pies are most easily frozen in foil containers which can be used in the oven for final cooking. If a bottom crust is used, sogginess will be prevented if the bottom pastry is brushed with melted butter or lard just before filling. Pies should be reheated at 400°F/200°C/Gas Mark 6 for the required time, according to size; they should not be stored longer than 2 months.

Hot Water Crust Pies

These are normally eaten cold, and can be frozen baked or unbaked; but there are obvious risks attached to freezing them. The pastry is made with hot water, and the pie must be completely baked *and cooled* before freezing; and the jelly must only be added just before the pie is to be served. The easiest way to do this is to freeze the stock separately at the time of making the pie, and when the pie is thawing (which takes about 4 hours) the partially-thawed pie can be filled with boiling stock through the hole in the crust (which will speed up the thawing process). Another method involves freezing the pie unbaked, partially thawing it and then baking it. However, this means that the uncooked meat is in contact with the warm uncooked pastry during the making process, and unless the pie is very carefully handled while cooling, there is every risk of dangerous organisms entering the meat.

It seems better therefore to avoid freezing game or pork pies made with this type of pastry.

Open Tarts
Tarts with only a bottom crust can be filled and frozen very successfully. They are better frozen before wrapping to avoid spoiling the surface of the filling during packing.

Pizza
Bought or home-made pizzas can be frozen, and are useful for entertaining and for snack meals. The pizza is best frozen on a flat foil plate on which it can be baked, wrapped in foil for storage. Anchovies should be omitted from the topping if possible as their saltiness may cause rancidity in the fatty cheese during storage; they can be added at the reheating stage. Fresh herbs should be used rather than dried. To serve, unwrap and thaw at room temperature for 1 hour, then bake at 375°F/190°C/ Gas Mark 5 for 25 minutes, and serve very hot.

Quiches
Open savoury flans or quiches made with short pastry are best completed and baked before freezing. They should be frozen without wrapping to avoid spoiling the surface, then wrapped in foil or polythene for storage, or packed in boxes to avoid damage. It is easier to bake and freeze these flans in foil cases, but this does not give much depth of filling, so that it is preferable to prepare them in flan rings, freeze unwrapped, and pack in boxes to avoid breaking the sides. They should be thawed in loose wrappings at room temperature to serve cold, but taste better if reheated. The traditional Quiche Lorraine freezes well, and spinach, shellfish and mushroom flans are also good. Leftover meat, fish or vegetables can also be bound with a savoury sauce and frozen in a pastry case.

Flan Cases
Unfilled flan cases can be frozen baked or unbaked. Unbaked cases should be frozen in flan rings. Baked cases are fragile, and are best packed in boxes to avoid crushing. Baked cases are the most useful to keep in the freezer as a meal can be produced more quickly with them. Baked cases should be thawed in their wrappings at room temperature before filling (about 1 hour should be enough); but a hot filling can be used when the case is taken from the freezer and the whole flan then heated in a slow oven.

Flans
Filled flans with open tops are best completed and baked before freezing, whether they are savoury or sweet. They should be frozen without wrapping to avoid spoiling the surface, then wrapped in foil or polythene for storage, or packed in boxes to avoid damage. Custard fillings should be avoided; so should meringue toppings which toughen and dry during storage. A meringue topping can be added just before serving. Thaw flans in loose wrappings at room temperature for 2 hours to serve cold, or reheat if required. Storage time: 2 months with fresh fillings; 1 month if made with leftover meat or vegetables.

Preparation for Freezing Sandwiches
Every filling keeps for a different length of time; so the best general rule is not to store any sandwiches in the freezer for longer than 4 weeks. Sandwiches should be packaged in groups of six or eight rather than individually; an extra slice or crust of bread at each end of the package will help to prevent them drying out.

Avoid fillings which contain cooked egg whites, which become dry and tough with freezing. Also avoid raw vegetables such as celery, lettuce, tomatoes and carrots, and salad cream or mayonnaise which will curdle and separate when frozen and soak into the bread when thawed. To prevent fillings seeping through, butter the bread liberally; this is easier to do if the bread is one day old.

Give variety to sandwiches by using a number of breads. Whole wheat, rye, pumpernickel and fruit breads are all excellent (the brown breads are particularly good for fish fillings, and the fruit bread for cheese and sweet fillings).

Sandwiches should not be frozen against the freezer wall as it will result in uneven thawing. Put the packages a few inches from the wall of the freezer, and see that the crusty edges of the sandwiches are towards the wall. Sandwiches should be defrosted in their wrappings at room temperature for four hours.

When quantities of sandwiches must be prepared, an assembly-line technique will speed up matters. Try doing them this way:
(a) Soften butter or margarine (but do not melt).

Leftover meat can be frozen and used later to make individual meat pies which are ideal for buffets and picnics.

Pizza

(b) Prepare fillings and refrigerate ready for use.

(c) Assemble wrapping materials.

(d) Assemble breads and cut (or split rolls or baps).

(e) Spread bread slices, going right to the edge to prevent fillings soaking in.

(f) Spread fillings evenly on bread to ensure even thawing time.

(g) Close and stack sandwiches.

(h) Cut with a sharp knife (sandwiches are best left in rather large portions, such as half slices) and leave crusts on.

(i) Wrap sandwiches tightly in Cellophane, then in foil or other moisture-vapour-proof wrap. With an inner wrapping, the other covering may be removed and retained at home and the neat inner package taken in a lunch box for thawing.

(j) Label and freeze.

These fillings are very satisfactory:

Cheese Cream cheese with olives and peanuts
Cream cheese with chutney
Cream cheese with chopped dates, figs or prunes
Cottage cheese with orange marmalade or apricot jam
Blue cheese with roast beef
Blue cheese with chopped cooked bacon
Cheddar cheese and chopped olives or chutney
Fish Mashed sardines, hard-boiled egg yolk and a squeeze of lemon juice
Minced shrimps, crab or lobster with cream cheese and lemon juice
Tuna with chutney
Canned salmon with cream cheese and lemon juice
Meat and Poultry Sliced meat such as tongue, corned beef, luncheon meat and chutney
Sliced roast beef with horseradish sauce
Sliced roast lamb with mint jelly
Sliced chicken or turkey with ham and chutney
Minced ham with chopped pickled cucumber and cream cheese

Open Freezing Baked Goods

It is preferable to freeze iced cakes and delicate pies before packaging them. They can be frozen on metal or plastic trays, and then packed in polythene or foil, or in a rigid box to prevent crushing.

Babas and Savarins
Preparation
(a) If syrup has been poured on to cake, pack in leakproof container. (b) Pack cake without syrup in foil or polythene.
To serve
(a) Thaw (without wrappings) at room temperature. (b) Thaw without wrappings at room temperature, and pour on warm syrup.
High Quality Storage Life   3 months

Biscuits
Preparation
(a) Make dough and form into cylinder about 2 in/5 cm diameter. Wrap in foil or polythene. (b) Bake biscuits. Pack carefully in boxes to avoid crushing. Biscuits keep well in tins, so freezer space need not be wasted.
To serve
(a) Thaw in wrappings in refrigerator for 45 minutes. Cut in slices and bake at 375°F/190°C/Gas Mark 5 for 10 minutes. (b) Thaw in wrappings at room temperature for 1 hour. Baked biscuits may be rather soft when thawed.
High Quality Storage Life (a) 2 months, (b) 4 months

Bread (Baked)
Preparation
Wrap in foil or polythene bags.
To serve
(a) Thaw in wrappings at room temperature for 3–6 hours, or in refrigerator overnight. (b) Put frozen load in moderate oven (400°F/200°C/Gas Mark 6) for 45 minutes.
High Quality Storage Life 4 weeks (plain bread); 6 weeks (enriched bread); 1 week (crisp-crusted bread).

Bread Dough
Preparation
(a) Form kneaded dough into a ball. Put in lightly greased polythene bag. Seal tightly and freeze at once. (b) Put dough in a large lightly greased polythene bag; tie loosely at top and leave to rise. Turn on to floured surface, knock back and knead until firm. Replace in polythene bag, seal tightly and freeze at once.

To serve
Unseal bag, and tie loosely at the top to allow space for rising. Thaw 6 hours at room temperature or overnight in refrigerator. Knock back, shape, rise and bake.
High Quality Storage Life   (a) 8 weeks (plain dough); 5 weeks (enriched dough); (b) 3 weeks.

Bread (Fruit and Nut)
Preparation
Do not overbake. Cool quickly. Pack in polythene bags.
To serve
Thaw in wrappings at room temperature. Slice while partly frozen to prevent crumbling.
High Quality Storage Life   2 months

Bread (Part-baked)
Preparation
Leave in wrapper and put into polythene bag. Seal and freeze at once.
To serve
Put frozen loaf in hot oven (425°F/220°C/Gas Mark 7) for 30 minutes. Cool 2 hours before cutting.
High Quality Storage Life   4 months

Bread (Sliced)
Preparation
Leave in wrapper and put in polythene bags. Seal and freeze at once.
To serve
(a) Thaw in wrappings at room temperature for 3–6 hours, or in refrigerator overnight. (b) Separate frozen slices with a knife and toast at once.
High Quality Storage Life   4 weeks

Brioche
Preparation
Pack immediately after baking and cooling in polythene bags.
To serve
Thaw in wrappings at room temperature for 30 minutes, and heat in oven or under grill, with or without filling.
High Quality Storage Life   2 months

Cake (Butter-iced)
Preparation
Put together cake layers with butter icing, and ice top with butter icing. Do not add decorations. Fast-freeze on a tray without wrappings. When frozen, pack in box, or in foil or polythene bag.
To serve
Remove wrappings and thaw at room temperature for 1½ hours. Add decorations.
High Quality Storage Life   4 months

Cake (Sponge)

Preparation

Sponges made with and without fat freeze equally well. Pack in layers with greaseproof paper or Clingfilm between. Pack in foil or polythene bag.

To serve

Thaw in wrappings at room temperature for 1½ hours.

High Quality Storage Life   4 months (with fat); 10 months (fatless).

Cake (Light Fruit)

Preparation

A light fruit cake, such as Dundee or sultana cake, will freeze well. Wrap in foil or polythene bag.

To serve

Thaw in wrappings at room temperature for 2 hours.

High Quality Storage Life   4 months

Cakes (Slab)

Preparation

Light fruit cakes, flavoured cakes (e.g. chocolate), gingerbread and spicecakes may be frozen in their baking tins, wrapped in foil or polythene.

To serve

Thaw in wrappings at room temperature for 1½ hours. Ice if required and cut in pieces.

High Quality Storage Life 4 months (fruit and flavoured); 2 months (ginger and spice).

Cakes (Small)

Preparation

Cakes made in bun tins, paper or foil cases can be frozen plain or iced. (a) Pack plain cakes in usable quantities in polythene bags. (b) Pack iced cakes in boxes layered with greaseproof paper or Clingfilm. Iced cakes are best fast-frozen on tray before packing.

To serve

(a) Thaw in wrappings at room temperature for 1 hour. (b) Remove wrappings and thaw at room temperature for 1 hour.

High Quality Storage Life 4 months

Cake (Rich Fruit)

Preparation

This type of cake will keep well in a tin, so freezer space should not be wasted. If a rich fruit cake is to be frozen, wrap in foil or polythene bag.

To serve

Thaw in wrappings at room temperature for 2 hours.

High Quality Storage Life 10 months

Choux Pastry, Éclairs and Cream Buns

Preparation

(a) Bake éclairs or cream buns. Freeze without filling or icing. Pack in boxes or bags. (b) Fill cases with ice cream. Freeze unwrapped on trays. Pack in boxes.

To Serve

(a) Thaw in wrappings at room temperature for 2 hours. Fill and ice. (b) Thaw at room temperature for 10 minutes. Pour over chocolate or toffee sauce.

High Quality Storage Life 1 month

Croissants

Preparation

Pack immediately after baking and cooling. Pack in bags, or in boxes to avoid crushing and flaking.

To serve

Thaw in wrappings at room temperature for 30 minutes, and heat in oven or under grill.

High Quality Storage Life 2 months

Crumpets

Preparation

Pack in usable quantities in polythene bags.

To serve

Thaw in wrappings at room temperature for 30 minutes, then toast.

High Quality Storage Life 10 months

Danish Pastries

Preparation

Prepare un-iced or with a light water icing. Pack in foil trays with lids, or in boxes to prevent crushing.

To serve

Remove wrappings and thaw at room temperature for 1 hour. Heat lightly if liked.

High Quality Storage Life 2 months

Doughnuts

Preparation

Ring doughnuts freeze better than jam doughnuts which may become soggy. Drain well from fat, and do not roll in sugar. Pack in polythene bags.

To serve

Heat frozen doughnuts at 400°F/200°C/Gas Mark 6 for 8 minutes, then roll in sugar.

High Quality Storage Life 1 month

Drop Scones

Preparation

Cool thoroughly before packing. Pack in boxes, foil or bags.

To serve

Thaw in wrappings at room temperature for 1 hour.

High Quality Storage Life 2 months

Muffins

Preparation
Pack in usable quantities in polythene bags.
To serve
Thaw in wrappings at room temperature for 30 minutes, then toast.
High Quality Storage Life   10 months

Pancakes

Preparation
Cool thoroughly before packing. Put layers of greaseproof paper or Cellophane between large thin pancakes. Wrap in foil or polythene.
To serve
Thaw in wrappings at room temperature and separate. Heat in low oven, or on a plate over steam, covered with a cloth.
High Quality Storage Life   2 months

Pastry (Slab)

Preparation
Roll pastry, form into a square and wrap in grease-proof paper. Overwrap in foil or polythene. Pack in usable quantities (i.e. 8 oz/225 g or 1 lb/450 g).
To serve
Thaw at room temperature for 2 hours. Eat freshly baked.
High Quality Storage Life   4 months

Pastry Cases

Preparation
Make up flan cases, patty cases and vol-au-vent cases. Use foil containers if possible. (a) Freeze unbaked cases packed in foil or polythene. (b) Bake cases and pack in boxes to prevent crushing.
To serve
Thaw unbaked cases at room temperature for 1 hour before baking. (a) Thaw baked cases at room temperature before filling. (b) Put hot filling into frozen cases and heat in oven.
High Quality Storage Life   4 months

Rolls and Buns

Preparation
Pack in polythene bags in usable quantities. Seal and freeze at once.
To serve
(a) Thaw in wrappings at room temperature for 1½ hours. (b) Put frozen rolls or buns in foil in a hot oven (450°F/230°C/Gas Mark 8) for 15 minutes.
High Quality Storage Life   4 weeks

Rolls (Part-baked)

Preparation
Leave in wrapper and put into polythene bag. Seal and freeze at once.

To serve
Put frozen rolls in moderate oven (400°F/200°C/Gas Mark 6) for 15 minutes.
High Quality Storage Life   4 months

Sandwiches

Preparation
Avoid fillings of cooked egg whites, salad dressings, mayonnaise, raw vegetables or jam. Spread bread with butter. Pack in groups of six or eight sandwiches, with an extra crust at each end to prevent drying out. Keep crusts on, and do not cut sandwiches in pieces. Wrap in foil or polythene and seal tightly.
To serve
(a) Thaw in wrappings in refrigerator for 12 hours, or at room temperature for 4 hours. Trim crusts and cut in pieces. (b) Put frozen sandwiches under grill to thaw while toasting.
High Quality Storage Life   1 month

Sandwiches (Open)

Preparation
Butter bread thickly. Make up without salad garnishes, open freeze and pack in single layer in rigid plastic box.
To serve
Thaw at room temperature for 2 hours. Garnish with salad and dressings.
High Quality Storage Life   1 week

Bread rolls

Sandwiches (Pinwheel, Club and Ribbon)
Preparation
Prepare but do not cut in pieces. Wrap tightly in foil.
To serve
Thaw in wrappings in refrigerator for 12 hours, or at room temperature for 4 hours. Cut in pieces.
High Quality Storage Life   1 month

Sandwiches (Rolled)
Preparation
Flatten bread with rolling pin to ease rolling. Butter well and wrap around filling. Pack closely together in box to prevent unrolling.
To serve
Thaw in wrappings in refrigerator for 12 hours, or at room temperature for 4 hours.
High Quality Storage Life   1 month

Scones
Preparation
Pack in usable quantities in polythene bags.
To serve
(a) Thaw in wrappings at room temperature for 1 hour. (b) Heat frozen scones (with a covering of foil) at 350°F/180°C/Gas Mark 4 for 10 minutes.
High Quality Storage Life   2 months

Waffles
Preparation
Do not brown too much. Cool and pack in usable quantities.
To serve
Heat frozen waffles under grill or in oven until crisp.
High Quality Storage Life   2 months

Yeast
Preparation
Weigh into $\frac{1}{4}$ oz/7 g, $\frac{1}{2}$ oz/15 g or 1 oz/25 g cubes. Wrap cubes in polythene and label carefully. Pack in box.
To serve
Thaw 30 minutes at room temperature. Frozen yeast may be grated coarsely for immediate use.
High Quality Storage Life   6 months

Freezing Cooked Dishes

Cooked meals which can be used straight from the freezer without further cooking are very useful. Strict hygiene must be observed in preparing cooked food for the freezer, and only good-quality raw materials should be used. Cooked food must be cooled quickly by standing the container in cold water and ice cubes. Surplus fat should be removed after cooling and before freezing. Fried foods must be well drained on absorbent paper, and must be very cold before packing to avoid sogginess. Dishes such as pies, piped potatoes and decorated puddings should be frozen before wrapping to avoid damage to the surface of the food.

Preparation for Freezing Soup

Besides completed soups, meat, chicken and fish stock can all be frozen to use as a basis for fresh soups. These stocks should be strained, cooled and defatted, and packed into cartons with headspace. They are best thawed in a saucepan over low heat.

Soup which is thickened with ordinary flour tends to curdle on reheating, so cornflour is best as a thickening agent; it gives a creamy result. Rice flour can be used, but makes the soup glutinous. Porridge oats can be used for thicker meat soups. Starchy foods such as rice, pasta, barley and potatoes become slushy when frozen in liquid, and should only be added during the final reheating after freezing. It is also better to omit milk or cream from frozen soups, as results with these ingredients are variable; they, too, can be added when reheating.

Soup to be frozen should be cooled, and surplus fat removed as this will separate in storage and may cause off-flavours. Soup should be frozen in leak-proof containers, allowing $\frac{1}{2}$ in/1·25 cm headspace for wide-topped containers and $\frac{3}{4}$ in/2 cm headspace for narrow-topped containers. Rigid plastic containers are useful for storage; a very large quantity of soup can be frozen in a bread tin or in freezer boxes lined with foil; the solid block can then be wrapped in foil and stored like a brick.

Soup should not be stored for longer than 2 months. It will thicken during freezing, and allowance should be made for this in the recipe so that additional liquid can be added on reheating without spoiling the soup. Seasoning can cause off-flavours, so it is best to season after thawing. Clear soups can be heated in a saucepan over low heat, but cream soups should be heated in a double boiler and beaten well to keep them smooth.

Soup Garnishes

Herbs and croûtons can be frozen to give an attractive finish to soups, even when time is limited.

Herb Cubes

Herbs such as parsley and chives should be chopped and packed in ice cube trays with a little water, then each frozen cube wrapped in foil. The herb cubes can be reheated in the soup.

Croûtons and Cheese Croûtons

Croûtons can be prepared from lightly-toasted $\frac{1}{2}$ in/ 1·25 cm slices of bread which are then cut in cubes and dried out in an oven set at 350°F/180°C/Gas Mark 4. They are best packed in small polythene bags and thawed in their wrappings at room temperature, but they can be reheated if preferred. As a variation, the bread can be toasted on one side only and the other side can be spread with grated cheese mixed with a little melted butter, egg yolk and seasoning; this is then toasted and the bread cut in cubes before packing.

Preparation for Freezing of Cooked Meat

Time can be saved by preparing meat dishes which can be frozen, then eaten cold or reheated after thawing. Pre-cooked joints, steaks and chops do not freeze successfully, since the outer surface sometimes develops an off-flavour, and reheating dries out the meat. Fried meats also tend to toughness, dryness and rancidity when frozen. Cold meat can however be frozen in slices, with or without sauce. Any combination dishes of meat and vegetables should include the vegetables when they are slightly undercooked, to avoid softness on reheating. In addition to casseroles and stews, good cooked dishes for freezing include cottage pie, galantines and meat loaves, meat balls, meat sauces, and meat pies. It is very important that all cooked meats should be cooled quickly before freezing. Where ingredients such as meat and gravy are to be combined, they should be thoroughly chilled separately before mixing; for instance hot gravy should not be poured over cold meat.

Preparation for Freezing of Cooked Poultry
Old birds such as boiling chickens are best if frozen when cooked, with the meat stripped from the bones. This meat can then be frozen or made at once into pies or casseroles, while the carcass can be simmered in the cooking liquid to make strong stock for freezing. Slices of cooked poultry can be frozen on their own or in a sauce (the latter is preferable to prevent drying out). If the meat is frozen without sauce, slices should be divided by sheets of Clingfilm and then closely packed together to exclude air. Roast and fried poultry frozen to be eaten cold are not particularly successful; on thawing they tend to exude moisture and be flabby.

Sliced Meat and Poultry
Cold poached, boiled or steamed meat and poultry can well be frozen in slices to serve cold. Slices should be at least $\frac{1}{4}$ in/6 mm thick, separated by Clingfilm or greaseproof paper, and must be packed tightly to avoid surfaces drying. They can then be put into cartons or bags. They should be thawed for 3 hours in a refrigerator in their container, then separated and placed on absorbent paper to remove any moisture. They are good; only ham and pork will lose colour when frozen like this.

It is preferable to freeze meat and poultry slices in gravy or sauce to make them keep their juiciness. The liquid may be thickened with cornflour, and both the meat and the gravy or sauce should be cooled quickly, separately, before packing. These slices are best packaged in foil containers, covered with a lid, and this can save time in reheating as the container can go straight into the oven, keeping the meat moist. These frozen slices in gravy should be heated for 30 minutes at 350°F/180°C/Gas Mark 4.

Casseroles
Casseroled meat and poultry is very useful to keep in the freezer. It is good sense to double the quantity of a casserole, using half when fresh and freezing the second half. For freezing, vegetables should be slightly undercooked in the casserole; pasta, rice, barley or potatoes should not be included or they will go slushy; onions, garlic and herbs should only be used sparingly, or should be added during reheating; sauces should be thickened with tomato purée, vegetable purée or cornflour, to avoid curdling on reheating. Oven-to-freezer casseroles can well be used if they are of the type advertised for the purpose, and they can be returned straight to the oven for reheating. Other oven-glass containers should be allowed to cool before placing in the freezer, and should be thawed before returning to the oven for serving. Casseroles and stews are very successful when frozen in foil containers which can be used in the oven, or in foil-lined containers so that the foil can be formed into a parcel for freezing, and the contents returned to the original container for heating and serving. If frozen in cartons, the dishes can be transferred to ovenware, or reheated in a double boiler, or even over direct heat if curdling is not likely to occur.

Galantines and Meat Loaves
Galantines are most easily used if cooked before freezing, ready to serve cold. They can be prepared directly in loaf tins, then turned out, wrapped and frozen. Meat loaves can be frozen uncooked. This is made easy if the mixture is packed into loaf tins lined with foil, the foil then being formed into a parcel for freezing; the frozen meat loaf can be returned to the original tin for baking.

For cold serving, any of these compact meats can be packed in slices, divided by cellophane or greaseproof paper, and re-formed into a loaf shape for freezing. Slices can be separated while still frozen and thawed quickly on absorbent paper.

Pâtés
Pâtés made from liver, game or poultry, freeze extremely well. They can be packed in individual pots ready for serving, or cooked in loaf tins or terrines, then turned out and wrapped in foil for easy storage. Pâtés containing strong seasoning, herbs or garlic should be carefully overwrapped.

Any pâté which has exuded fat or excess juices during cooking must be carefully cooled and the excess fat or jelly scraped off before freezing. To serve, thaw small individual containers at room temperature for 1 hour. Thaw large pâtés in their wrappings in the refrigerator for 6 hours, or at room temperature for 3 hours, and use immediately after thawing. High quality storage life: 1 month. Pâtés can also be made with smoked fish, such as kippers or cod's roe. These are best prepared in small containers, well overwrapped. Any fish pâté should be thawed in a refrigerator for 3 hours.

Spaghetti served with kidneys makes an interesting alternative to more traditional pasta dishes.

Cooked Fish

Fish should never be overcooked, and the time taken to reheat a cooked fish dish will not only spoil flavour and rob the fish of any nutritive value, but will also take as long as the original cooking. Left-over cooked fish can however be frozen in the form of a fish pie, fish cakes, or a ready-to-eat dish in sauce. Raw fish can be frozen, coated in batter or egg and breadcrumbs and fried; but it tends to go rancid, and will take about 15 minutes to reheat, so there is little advantage in freezing it.

Pasta

Pasta such as spaghetti and macaroni can be frozen successfully to be used with a variety of sauces. Composite meals such as macaroni cheese can also be frozen when cooked. Pasta shapes can be frozen to use with soup; but they should not be frozen in liquid as they become slushy, so are most conveniently added to the soup during the reheating period.

Pasta should be slightly undercooked, in boiling salted water. After thorough draining, it should be cooled under cold running water in a sieve, then shaken as dry as possible, packed into polythene bags, and frozen. To serve, the pasta is put into a pan of boiling water and brought back to the boil, then simmered until just tender, the time depending on the state in which it has been frozen. Composite dishes can be reheated in a double boiler or in the oven under a foil lid. High quality storage life: 1 month.

While it may not save much time to prepare pasta specially for the freezer, it is useful to be able to save excess quantities prepared for a meal, or to turn them into a composite dish for the freezer.

Sauces

Sweet and savoury sauces can well be frozen, and are useful for emergency meals. They can be in the form of complete sauces such as a meat sauce to use with spaghetti or rice, or you can freeze a basic white or brown sauce to be used with other ingredients when reheated. Sauces for freezing are best thickened by reduction or with cornflour, as flour-thickened sauces are likely to curdle when reheated. Only mayonnaise and custard sauces cannot be frozen, since the ingredients freeze at different temperatures and give unsatisfactory results.

Sauces can be stored in large quantities in cartons, or in 'brick' form using loaf tins. Small quantities can be frozen in ice cube trays, then wrapped individually in foil and packed in quantities in bags for easy storage.

Flans (Savoury and Sweet)

Preparation
Prepare and bake flan, and finish completely. Freeze on a tray without wrappings. Wrap in foil or polythene, or pack in box to prevent damage.
To serve
Thaw in loose wrappings at room temperature for 2 hours. Reheat if required.
High Quality Storage Life   2 months (fresh filling); 1 month (leftover meat or vegetables)

Pasta

Preparation
Slightly undercook macaroni, spaghetti or other pasta. Drain thoroughly and cool. Pack in polythene bags in usable quantities.

To serve
Plunge into boiling water. Bring water to the boil and cook pasta until just tender.
High Quality Storage Life   1 month

Rice

Preparation
Slightly undercook rice. Drain thoroughly and pack in polythene bags in usable quantities.
To serve
(a) Plunge into boiling water. Bring water to boil and cook rice until just tender. (b) Reheat in melted butter in a thick pan. (c) Reheat in a shallow pan in a low oven.
High Quality Storage Life   1 month

Rice

Freezing Puddings

Preparation for Freezing of Puddings
A wide variety of puddings can be frozen and are useful for emergency use; this can also be a way of storing surplus fruit in a convenient form. Puddings which can be frozen include obvious items such as

ice cream and pies, and pancakes and sponge cakes which can be combined quickly with fruit, cream or sauces to make complete puddings. Steamed puddings can also be frozen, together with fruit crumbles, gelatine sweets, cold soufflés and mousses and cheesecakes. Milk puddings do not freeze well, however, since they become mushy or curdle.

Baked and Steamed Puddings

These can be made from almost all standard cake and pudding recipes, and are most easily made in foil containers which can be used for freezing and for heating. It is better not to put jam or syrup in the bottom of these puddings before cooking, as they become soggy on thawing, but dried fruit, fresh fruits and nuts can be added. Highly-spiced puddings may develop off-flavours.

Suet puddings containing fresh fruit can be frozen raw or cooked. It is more useful, however, to cook them before freezing, since only a short time need then be allowed for reheating before serving. Puddings made from cake mixtures, or any traditional sponge or suet puddings, can also be frozen raw or cooked. Cake mixtures can be used to top such fruits as apples, plums, gooseberries and apricots; these are just as easily frozen raw since the complete cooking time in the oven is only a little longer than reheating time. This also applies to fruit puddings with a crumble topping.

Fruit Puddings

It is useful to use some fruit to make prepared puddings for the freezer. Fruit in syrup can be flavoured with wine or liqueurs and needs no further cooking; this is particularly useful for such fruits as pears and peaches which are difficult to freeze well in their raw state.

Gelatine Puddings

Many cold puddings involve the use of gelatine. When gelatine is frozen in a creamy mixture, it is entirely successful, although clear jellies are not recommended for the freezer. The ice crystals formed in freezing break up the structure of the jelly, and while it retains its setting quality, the jelly becomes granular and uneven and loses clarity. This granular effect is masked in such puddings as mousses.

Pudding Sauces

A supply of sweet sauces such as fruit sauce or chocolate sauce can be usefully frozen for use with puddings or ices. These are best prepared and frozen in small containers, and reheated in a double boiler.

Mousses and Cold Soufflés
Preparation
Prepare in serving dishes if these are freezer-tested.
To serve
Thaw in refrigerator for 8 hours.
High Quality Storage Life   1 month

Baked and Steamed Puddings
Preparation
Prepare standard sponge pudding or cake mixture recipes. Use with jam, fresh or dried fruit. Steam or bake in foil containers. Cool completely. Cover with foil or pack in polythene bag.
To serve
Thaw at room temperature for 2 hours. Steam for 45 minutes.
High Quality Storage Life   4 months

Freezing Snacks and Starters

Appetizers
Preparation
Wrap rindless bacon round chicken livers, cocktail sausages, seafood or cooked prunes. Secure with cocktail sticks. Fast-freeze on trays. Transfer to polythene bags for storage.
To serve
Cook frozen appetisers under grill or in hot oven until bacon is crisp.
High Quality Storage Life   2 weeks

Canapés
Preparation
Cut day-old bread into shapes, but do not use toast or fried bread. Spread butter to edge of bread. Add toppings, but avoid hard-boiled eggs or mayonnaise. Aspic becomes cloudy on thawing. Fast-freeze unwrapped on trays. Pack in boxes for storage.
To serve
Thaw on dish 1 hour before serving. Garnish if necessary.
High Quality Storage Life   2 weeks

Dips
Preparation
Make dips with a base of cottage or cream cheese. Avoid mayonnaise, hard-boiled egg whites or crisp vegetables. Pack in waxed or rigid plastic containers. Overwrap if dips contain garlic or onion.
To serve
Thaw in containers at room temperature for 5 hours. Blend in mayonnaise, egg whites or vegetables if necessary.
High Quality Storage Life   1 month

Canapés

Flavoured Butters
Preparation
(a) Fast-freeze butter balls or curls on trays. Transfer to polythene bags for storage. (b) Cream butter with herbs, lemon juice, or shellfish. Form into cylinders and wrap in greaseproof paper and polythene.
To serve
(a) Thaw in serving dishes at room temperature for 1 hour. (b) Cut in slices to put on hot meat or fish.
High Quality Storage Life   6 months (unsalted); 3 months (salted)

High Quality Storage Life

It is important that food stored in the freezer should not remain static; a good turnover should be maintained. Many foods can be stored for months in the freezer, but if they are kept too long colour, flavour and texture suffer. 'High Quality Storage Life' is the longest time food should be stored so that it is still perfect in every way when used. Cooked dishes in particular should be used within this storage time. Commercially-frozen packs should not be stored for longer than 3 months, and ice cream is best stored for no longer than 1 month.

It is a waste of valuable freezer space to store food beyond the end of the recommended storage life.

Remember that the wrong packaging material, bad packing and air spaces in the packs will affect the keeping qualities of frozen food. Salt, spices, herbs, onion, garlic and fats also shorten the keeping time of foods as well as affecting flavours.

ITEM	HIGH QUALITY STORAGE LIFE NUMBER OF MONTHS
Meat	
Beef	12
Ham and Bacon (whole)	3
Ham and Bacon (sliced)	1
Lamb	9
Minced Beef	2
Offal	2
Pork	6
Sausages and Sausage Meat	1
Veal	9
Poultry	
Chicken	12
Duck	6
Giblets	3
Goose	6
Poultry Stuffing	1
Turkey	6
Game	
Feathered Game	10
Hare	6
Rabbit	6
Venison	12

ITEM	HIGH QUALITY STORAGE LIFE NUMBER OF MONTHS
Fish	
Oily Fish (Herring, Mackerel, Salmon, Trout)	2
Shellfish	1
White Fish (Cod, Haddock, Plaice, Sole)	6
Vegetables	
Asparagus	9
Beans	12
Brussels Sprouts	10
Carrots	10
Fresh Herbs	10
Part-Fried Chips	4
Peas	12
Spinach	12
Tomatoes	6
Fruit	
Apricots	6
Cherries	7
Currants	10
Fruit Juices	9
Fruit Purées	5
Gooseberries	10
Melon	9
Peaches	6
Plums	6
Raspberries	12
Rhubarb	12
Strawberries	12

ITEM	HIGH QUALITY STORAGE LIFE NUMBER OF MONTHS
Dairy Produce	
Double Cream	6
Eggs	12
Fresh Butter	6
Hard Cheese	3
Ice Cream	1
Salted Butter	3
Soft Cheese	6
Bakery Goods	
Baked Bread, Rolls and Buns	2
Breadcrumbs	3
Danish Pastry	1
Decorated Cakes	3
Fried Bread Shapes	1
Fruit Pies	6
Meat Pies	3
Pancakes (unfilled)	2
Pastry Cases	3
Pizza	1
Plain Cakes	6
Sandwiches	2
Savoury Flans	2
Unbaked Biscuits	4
Unbaked Bread, Rolls and Buns	2
Unbaked Cakes	2
Unbaked Pastry	3
Cooked Dishes	
Casseroles and Stews	2
Curry	2
Filled Pancakes	1
Fish Dishes	2
Meat in Sauce	2
Meat Loaf	1
Pâté	1
Roast Meat	1
Sauces	2
Soufflés and Mousses	2
Soup	2
Sponge Puddings	3
Stock	2

Foods to Avoid Freezing

Nearly all foods freeze well, but there are a few items to avoid completely, or to freeze only with great care. A few other foods cannot be frozen to eat raw, but can be used for cooking.

Here is a list of foods which are unsuitable for freezing:

Hard-boiled eggs (including Scotch eggs, eggs in pies and in sandwiches).

Soured cream and single cream (less than 40% butterfat) which separate.

Custards (including tarts). The custard mixture of eggs and milk can be frozen uncooked but there is little point in this.

Soft meringue toppings.

Mayonnaise and salad dressings.

Milk puddings.

Royal icing and frostings without fat.

Salad vegetables with a high water content, e.g. lettuce, watercress, radishes.

Old boiled potatoes (potatoes can be frozen mashed, roasted, baked or as chips).

Stuffed poultry (the storage life of stuffing is very short, compared with poultry).

Food with a high proportion of gelatine.

Whole eggs in shells which will crack (eggs can be frozen in packages).

Here is a list of foods to freeze with care:

Onions, garlic, spices and herbs. They sometimes get a musty flavour in cooked dishes in the freezer, and quantities should be reduced in such dishes as casseroles, and adjusted during reheating.

Careful packing will help to prevent these strong flavours spreading to other food, and a short storage life is recommended.

Rice, spaghetti and potatoes should only be frozen without liquid. They become mushy in liquid and should not be frozen in soups or stews.

Sauces and gravy are best thickened by reduction, or with tomato or vegetable purée. If flour is used, it must be reheated with great care, preferably in a double saucepan, to avoid separation. Cornflour can be used but gives a glutinous quality. Egg and cream thickening should be added after freezing.

Bananas, apples, pears, whole melons and avocadoes cannot be successfully frozen whole to eat raw. They can be prepared in various ways for freezer storage (although pears are never very satisfactory). Bananas are not worth while as they are in season at a reasonable price throughout the year.

Cabbage cannot be frozen successfully to eat raw, and is not worth freezing as it occupies valuable freezer space. Red cabbage may be useful to keep frozen, as it has a short season and is never very plentiful.

Celery and chicory cannot be frozen to eat raw. They are useful to freeze in liquid to serve as vegetables. Celery can be used in stews or soup.

Tomatoes cannot be frozen to eat raw, but are invaluable in the freezer to use for soups, stews and sauces, or to freeze as purée or juice.

Milk must be homogenised and packed in waxed cartons. It is hardly worth bothering about as various types of milk can be stored without refrigeration.

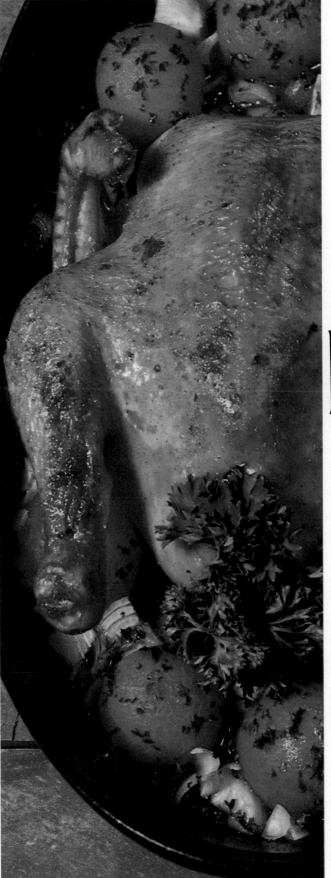

Complete
Freezer
Book
Part 11

Soups

Celery Soup

1 lb/450 g celery
1 small onion
2 pints/1 litre chicken stock
1 tablespoon chopped parsley

Cut the celery into short lengths and chop the onion. Bring the stock to the boil, and add the celery, onion and parsley. Cover and simmer for 30 minutes. Sieve or liquidise until smooth, and cool. Pack into a rigid container, leaving headspace, and freeze.

To serve
Reheat gently until hot. Whip 2 egg yolks with $\frac{1}{4}$ pint/125 ml single cream. Add a little of the soup to the cream mixture and stir well. Gradually add the cream mixture to the soup and heat gently, but do not boil. Season to taste and serve hot with a garnish of chopped parsley.
High Quality Storage Life   2 months

Green Pea Soup

2 lb/1 kg green peas
1 oz/25 g butter
1 small onion
1 small lettuce
pinch of mixed herbs
3 pints/1·5 litres chicken stock
salt and pepper

Frozen peas may be used for this soup, or shelled fresh peas. Put the peas, butter, finely chopped onion, shredded lettuce and herbs in a pan with a tight-fitting lid and simmer for 10 minutes. Add the stock, salt and pepper and simmer for 1 hour. Put through a sieve or blend until smooth, and cool. Pack in a rigid container, leaving headspace, to freeze.

To serve
Reheat gently and adjust seasoning to taste. Stir in 3 tablespoons single cream just before serving. If liked, fried or toasted bread cubes, or small pieces of crisp bacon make good garnishes.
High Quality Storage Life   2 months

Italian Tomato Soup

2 medium onions
1 garlic clove
2 tablespoons/30 ml olive oil
2 lb/1 kg ripe tomatoes
salt and pepper
1 teaspoon sugar
pinch of mint
pinch of basil
pinch of marjoram
2 pints/1 litre beef stock
For serving
2 oz/50 g cooked long-grain rice
1 oz/25 g grated Parmesan cheese

Chop the onions finely and crush the garlic. Cook them in the oil until soft and golden. Add the peeled tomatoes cut into pieces, with the salt, pepper, sugar and herbs. Cover with the stock and simmer for 30 minutes. Put through a sieve, cool and pack in a rigid container to freeze.

To serve
Reheat gently and add the cooked rice. Just before serving, sprinkle with cheese.
High Quality Storage Life   2 months

Kidney Soup

8 oz/225 g ox kidney
1 oz/25 g butter
1 small onion
2 pints/1 litre beef stock
1 carrot
sprig of parsley
sprig of thyme
1 bay leaf
salt and pepper
1 oz/25 g cornflour

Wash the kidney and cut in slices. Cook the kidney and sliced onion in the butter until the onion is soft and golden. Add the stock, chopped carrot, herbs and seasoning and simmer for 1½ hours. Put through a sieve, or blend in a liquidiser and return to the pan. Mix the cornflour with a little water and stir into the soup. Simmer for 5 minutes. Cool and pack into a rigid container, leaving headspace; freeze.
To serve
Reheat gently until hot, and stir in 2 tablespoons sherry just before serving.
High Quality Storage Life   2 months

Italian tomato soup is made from fresh, ripe tomatoes with a delicious flavouring of herbs and is served with a garnish of rice and grated cheese.

Leek soup, made with potatoes, forms a complete meal if served with toast or newly-baked bread

Leek Soup

4 large leeks
1 oz/25 g butter
3 pints/1·5 litres water or chicken stock
1 lb/450 g potatoes
salt and pepper
pinch of nutmeg

Remove the green tops from the leeks and wash the white parts very carefully. Cut them in thin rings and cook in the butter over low heat until they begin to soften. Add the water or stock, sliced potatoes and seasonings. Cover and simmer until the vegetables are soft. Cool, pack in a rigid container and freeze.

To serve
Reheat gently and just before serving stir in $\frac{1}{4}$ pint/ 125 ml single cream. Garnish with chopped parsley or chives if liked, and serve with cubes of toasted or fried bread, or with French bread.

High Quality Storage Life 2 months

Spring chicken soup is a
nourishing complete meal
which can be made richer
by adding egg thickening
after freezing.

Spring Chicken Soup

3 lb/1·5 kg chicken
2 sticks celery
1 leek
1 carrot
4 oz/100 g peas
salt and pepper

Remove the giblets from the chicken. Put the chicken into a saucepan, cover with water and bring to the boil. Reduce the heat and simmer for 1 hour. Remove the chicken from the cooking liquid and cut the flesh into neat pieces (some of the chicken breast could be used for another meal). Cut the celery and leek into neat pieces and slice the carrot into thin rings. Add to the cooking liquid with the chicken flesh and simmer for 15 minutes. Add the peas (which may be fresh or frozen) and simmer again for 5 minutes. Season lightly and then cool. Pour into a rigid container and freeze, leaving headspace.
To serve
Reheat gently, adjust seasoning and serve hot. For a richer soup, mix 2 egg yolks with a little milk and pour a little of the hot soup into this mixture. Stir the egg yolk mixture into the soup and heat gently but do not boil.
High Quality Storage Life   2 months

Carrot Soup

1 lb/450 g carrots
1 pint/500 ml water
1 oz/25 g butter
3 large tomatoes
salt and pepper

Scrape the carrots and cook for 30 minutes in the water. Drain, reserving the liquid, and then grate the carrots. Melt the butter and lightly cook the skinned and pipped tomatoes. Add the grated carrot and cook until all the butter is absorbed. Add the carrot cooking liquid and simmer for 30 minutes. Season lightly with salt and pepper and cool. Pack in a rigid container, leaving headspace, and freeze.
To serve
Reheat gently and when completely thawed add 1 pint/500 ml milk. Simmer until hot and adjust seasoning to taste, then garnish with chopped parsley.
High Quality Storage Life   2 months

Cock-a-Leekie Soup

1 boiling chicken
1 lb/450 g shin beef
6 leeks
1 small teaspoon black pepper
2 level teaspoons salt
4 oz/100 g prunes

Wipe the chicken inside and out and put into a large saucepan. Cut meat into small pieces. Clean and slice leeks thinly, using some of the green parts. Add salt and pepper and cover with cold water. Bring to simmering point and cook gently for 4 hours. Add the prunes and simmer 45 minutes. Take out the chicken and cut flesh into neat small pieces, return to saucepan and reheat. Pack into containers, leaving headspace, and freeze.
To serve
Reheat gently, adjusting seasoning.
High Quality Storage Life   2 months

Basic Chicken Stock

1 chicken carcass
2 pints/1 litre water
1 carrot
1 onion
1 stick celery
sprig of parsley
pinch of salt

Break up the carcass and put in a pan with sliced vegetables, water and salt. Simmer for 2 hours, strain and cool removing fat from the surface. Pack into containers, leaving headspace, and freeze.
To serve
Thaw in a saucepan over low heat and add to dishes as required.
High Quality Storage Life   2 months

Oxtail soup is delicious served with chunks of freshly baked French bread.

Oxtail Soup

1 oxtail
2½ pints/1½ litres water
2 carrots
2 onions
1 turnip
1 stick celery
1 oz/30 g pearl barley
salt

Wipe the oxtail and cut into pieces. Toss in a little seasoned flour and fry in a little butter for 10 minutes. Put in pan with water and simmer for 2 hours. Remove meat from bones and return to stock with vegetables, cut in neat pieces, and pearl barley and add seasoning. Simmer for 45 minutes and put through a sieve, or liquidise. Cool and remove fat from the top. Pack in containers, leaving headspace, and freeze.
To serve
Reheat gently in saucepan, adding ½ teaspoon Worcestershire sauce and ½ teaspoon lemon juice.
High Quality Storage Life   2 months

Turkey Soup

1 turkey carcass
cooked turkey giblets
giblet stock or gravy
1 onion
1 carrot
1 stick celery
1 bay leaf
1 strip of lemon rind
salt and pepper

Break up the carcass and put it with all the other ingredients into a large pan with water to cover. Simmer for 2 hours. Strain and cool. Remove excess fat, pack soup in rigid container, and freeze.
To serve
Reheat gently and adjust seasoning to taste, or use as a baste for other soups.
High Quality Storage Life   2 months

Hare soup is blended, after preparation, to make a delicious smooth-textured soup.

Hare Soup

1 hare
1 lb/450 g lean ham
1 medium onion
1 leek
1 carrot
parsley, thyme and marjoram
salt and pepper
3 blades of mace
6 pints/2½ litres beef stock
2 rolls
½ pint/250 ml port

Cut hare into joints and put into a pan with chopped ham and vegetables, herbs, salt and pepper, mace and stock. Simmer for 2½ hours. Remove meat from bones and put into blender with the ham, the crumbled rolls and some of the hare liquor which has been strained. Blend until smooth, then mix with remaining hare liquor and port, and simmer for 20 minutes. Cool. Pack in waxed or rigid containers, leaving headspace, and freeze.

To serve
Reheat gently in double boiler.
High Quality Storage Life   2 months

Beetroot Soup

12 oz/350 g cooked beetroot
1 medium onion
$\frac{3}{4}$ pint/375 ml chicken stock
3 celery leaves
$\frac{1}{2}$ teaspoon salt
pepper
1 teaspoon/7 g sugar
3 dessertspoons/30 ml lemon juice

Dice the beetroot and put into a liquidiser with the chopped onion, stock, celery, salt, pepper and sugar. Blend until the beetroot is finely chopped. Put into a pan and simmer for 10 minutes. Add the lemon juice and leave until cold. Pack into containers, leaving headspace, and freeze.
To serve
Reheat gently, or thaw and serve cold.
High Quality Storage Life   2 months

Onion Soup

$1\frac{1}{2}$ lb/675 g onions
2 oz/50 g butter
3 pints/$1\frac{1}{2}$ litres beef stock
salt and pepper
2 tablespoons/25 g cornflour

Slice the onion finely and cook gently in the butter until soft and golden. Add the stock and seasoning, bring to the boil, then simmer for 20 minutes. Thicken with cornflour mixed with a little water. Simmer a further 5 minutes. Cool and skim off any surplus fat. Pack into rigid containers, leaving headspace, and freeze.
To serve
Reheat gently, stirring well.
High Quality Storage Life   2 months

Pâtés

Cod's Roe Pâté

12 oz/350 g smoked cod's roe
¼ pint/125 ml double cream
1 garlic clove
juice of ½ lemon
2 teaspoons/10 ml olive oil
black pepper

Scrape the roe into a bowl and mix with the cream, crushed garlic, lemon juice and oil. Season to taste with pepper and mix well until the pâté is like thick cream. Pack into small containers and cover to freeze.
To serve
Thaw in refrigerator for 4 hours, stirring occasionally to blend ingredients. Serve with wedges of lemon and hot toast.
High Quality Storage Life   1 month

Kipper Mousse

10 oz/300 g kipper fillets
½ pint/250 ml single cream
1 oz/25 g butter
1 oz/25 g plain flour
½ pint/250 ml milk
salt and pepper
2 eggs
½ oz/15 g gelatine
juice of ½ lemon
2 tablespoons/30 ml water

Cook fresh or frozen kippers by grilling or boiling. Skin the fish and flake the flesh. Mix the kippers with a little of the cream and pound to a paste, adding remaining cream (or blend in a liquidiser). Melt the butter and stir in the flour. Cook for 1 minute and then gradually add the milk. Stir over low heat until smooth. Remove from heat, season and beat in egg yolks. Dissolve the gelatine in the lemon juice and water and heat until syrupy. Stir into the white sauce and leave to cool slightly before folding into the creamed kipper mixture. Whisk egg whites to soft peaks and fold into the kipper mixture. Turn into a 1½ pint/750 ml dish and leave until cold and set. Cover and freeze.
To serve
Thaw in the refrigerator for 4 hours and serve with thinly-sliced cucumber and brown bread and butter.
High Quality Storage Life   1 month

Sardine Pâté

8 oz/225 g canned sardines in oil
juice of ½ lemon
salt and pepper
2 oz/50 g melted butter

Bone the sardines and then mash them in a bowl with their skins and oil. For a really smooth pâté, put into a blender. Work in the lemon juice and season well. Press into a freezer-proof pot and cover with butter. Chill and then cover with foil and freeze.
To serve
Thaw in refrigerator for 6 hours to serve with toast.
High Quality Storage Life   1 month

Chicken Liver Pâté

8 oz/225 g chicken livers
3 oz/75 g fat bacon
1 small onion
2 garlic cloves
1 egg
1 oz/25 g butter
salt and pepper

Cut the livers into small pieces and chop the bacon and onion. Cook the bacon and onion in butter until just soft. Add the livers and cook gently for 10 minutes. Mince very finely and season. Add crushed garlic and beaten egg and put the mixture into individual foil containers. Stand the containers in a baking tin of water, cover and cook at 350°F/180°C/ Gas Mark 4 for 1 hour. Cool completely. Cover containers with foil to freeze.

To serve

Thaw containers in refrigerator for 3 hours and serve with toast.

High Quality Storage Life   1 month

Chunky Pâté

12 oz/350 g belly pork
12 oz/250 g bacon pieces
1½ oz/40 g crustless white bread
freshly ground black pepper
½ teaspoon sage
½ teaspoon mustard powder
1 egg
3 tablespoons/45 ml milk
4 oz/100 g liver sausage

Mince the pork, bacon and bread. Mix with the pepper, sage, mustard, egg and milk and beat well. Grease a 1 lb/450 g loaf tin and spread in half the meat mixture. Chop the liver sausage in small pieces and cover the meat mixture. Top with remaining meat mixture. Cover with foil and bake at 350°F/ 180°C/Gas Mark 4 for 45 minutes. Strain off excess fat. Continue cooking for 15 minutes. Cool in tin and turn out. Wrap in foil or polythene to freeze.

To serve

Thaw in refrigerator for 6 hours then cut in slices.

High Quality Storage Life   2 months

Liver Pâté

12 oz/350 g pig's liver
8 oz/225 g pork fat
5 anchovy fillets
1 small onion
2 oz/50 g dry breadcrumbs
½ pint/250 ml milk
1 oz/25 g butter
1 oz/25 g plain flour
1 egg
1 teaspoon salt
1 teaspoon pepper
1 teaspoon ground mixed spice
1 teaspoon ground cloves
½ teaspoon sugar
12 oz/350 g strips of pork fat

Liver pâté with a covering of thin slices of pork fat makes an excellent meal with salad and pickled cucumbers.

This Danish liver pâté is smooth, creamy and firm, and very easy to slice. The strips of pork fat should be cut very thinly for lining the container. Mince the liver, pork fat, anchovy fillets and onion with the fine blade three times. Soak the breadcrumbs in a little of the milk. Melt the butter, work in the flour and add the milk. Cook together, stirring well, to make a thick white sauce. Cool and stir in the egg and seasonings. Mix the sauce thoroughly into the liver mixture until smoothly blended, together with the breadcrumbs. Line 1½ lb/675 g tin or ovenware container with strips of pork fat so that they overlap slightly and cover the bottom and sides of the container. Put the liver mixture into the container and cover with strips of pork fat. Cover with a double thickness of cooking foil, and put the container into a baking tin half-full of water. Bake at 350°F/180°C/Gas Mark 4 for 1½ hours. Remove the foil and chill the pâté under weights. Turn out of the container and wrap in foil or polythene to freeze.

To serve

Unwrap and thaw in the refrigerator for 6 hours. Serve with salad or toast, or on open sandwiches, accompanied by pickled cucumbers.

High Quality Storage Life   2 months

Simple Pork Pâté

12 oz/350 g pig's liver
2 lb/1 kg belly pork
1 large onion
butter
bacon fat
1 large egg
½ oz/15 g plain flour
salt and pepper
pinch of ground nutmeg
1 tablespoon chopped parsley

Put the liver and pork through a coarse mincer. Chop the onion finely and soften in a little butter or bacon fat. Put the meat, onion and cooking juices, egg, flour, seasoning and parsley into a blender, and blend on maximum speed for 5 seconds. Put mixture into a greased loaf tin or ovenware dish, cover with foil and put into a roasting tin of water. Cook at 350°F/180°C/Gas Mark 4 for 1¾ hours. Cool under weights. Turn out and wrap in foil or polythene to freeze.
To serve
Thaw in refrigerator for 6 hours and cut in slices to serve with toast or salad.
High Quality Storage Life   2 months

Liver and Sausage Bake

8 oz/225 g pig's liver
8 oz/225 g sausages
1 oz/25 g butter
2 medium onions
8 oz/225 g tomatoes
salt and pepper
pinch of sage
½ pint/250 ml stock

Cut the liver into thin slices. Skin the sausages and cut in slices. Melt the butter and cook the sliced onions until soft but not brown. Drain off fat. Arrange onions, liver, sausages and sliced tomatoes in layers in a foil container, seasoning each layer with salt, pepper and sage. Pour over stock, cover and cook at 350°F/180°C/Gas Mark 4 for 30 minutes. Cool, cover with a lid and freeze.
To serve
Replace lid with foil and cook at 325°F/170°C/Gas Mark 3 for 1 hour.
High Quality Storage Life   2 months

Fish Dishes

Kipper and Cheese Pizza

2 oz/50 g margarine
8 oz/225 g self-raising flour
$\frac{1}{2}$ teaspoon salt
$\frac{1}{4}$ pint/125 ml milk
1 oz/25 g butter
8 oz/225 g onions
8 oz/225 g tomatoes
4 oz/100 g grated Cheddar cheese
8 oz/225 g kipper fillets

Rub the margarine into the sifted flour and salt and mix with milk to give a soft dough. Roll out to an 8 in/20 cm circle and put on a greased baking sheet. Melt the butter and fry the sliced onions until soft and golden. Spread on top of the dough. Top with sliced tomatoes and cheese. Thaw the kipper fillets and cut them into thin strips. Arrange on top and bake at 425°F/220°C/Gas Mark 7 for 20 minutes. Cool and wrap in foil to freeze.
To serve
Reheat at 350°F/180°C/Gas Mark 4 for 30 minutes.
High Quality Storage Life   1 month

Seafood Flan

8 oz/225 g shortcrust pastry
8 oz/225 g cod steaks
4 oz/100 g thawed frozen prawns
2 eggs
$\frac{1}{4}$ pint/125 ml milk
2 tablespoons chopped parsley
2 teaspoons/10 ml lemon juice
salt and pepper

Roll out the pastry to line an 8 in/20 cm flan ring. Prick with a fork and line with foil. Fill with baking beans and bake at 400°F/200°C/Gas Mark 6 for 15 minutes. Remove foil and beans. Cook the cod and flake coarsely. Put into the pastry case with the prawns. Beat the eggs and milk together, add parsley and lemon juice and season well with salt and pepper. Pour over the fish and bake at 350°F/180°C/Gas Mark 4 for 30 minutes. Cool and pack in foil to freeze.
To serve
Unwrap and reheat from frozen at 350°F/180°C/Gas Mark 4 for 30 minutes.
High Quality Storage Life   1 month

Fish Cakes

8 oz/225 g cooked white fish
8 oz/225 g mashed potatoes
2 teaspoons chopped parsley
1 oz/25 g melted butter
salt and pepper
beaten egg
breadcrumbs

Mix flaked fish, potatoes, parsley, melted butter, salt and pepper and bind with a little egg. Divide the mixture into 8 portions and form into flat cakes. Coat with egg and breadcrumbs and fry until golden. Cool quickly, open-freeze and pack in bags for storage.
To serve
Thaw by reheating in the oven or frying pan.
High Quality Storage Life   2 months

Smoked Haddock Cobbler

1 lb/450 g smoked haddock fillet
$\frac{3}{4}$ pint/375 ml milk
1 oz/25 g butter
1 oz/25 g plain flour
$1\frac{1}{2}$ tablespoons/22 ml lemon juice
2 tablespoons chopped parsley
salt and pepper
Topping
8 oz/225 g self-raising flour
$\frac{1}{4}$ teaspoon salt
2 oz/50 g butter
1 teaspoon mustard powder
3 oz/75 g grated Cheddar cheese
$\frac{1}{4}$ pint/125 ml milk

Poach the fish in the milk for 15 minutes and reserve the milk. Flake the fish. Melt the butter, stir in the flour and then the reserved milk. Return to the heat and stir until the sauce thickens. Add the flaked fish, lemon juice, parsley, salt and pepper. Spoon into a greased ovenware or freezer dish. Rub the butter into the sifted flour and salt until the mixture is like fine breadcrumbs. Stir in the mustard and 2 oz/50 g cheese. Add enough milk to mix to a soft light dough. Knead lightly and roll out to a rectangle about 9×4 in (22·5 $\times$ 10 cm). Divide into 6 rectangles and cut each in half diagonally to make triangles. Arrange, slightly overlapping, on top of fish mixture. Brush with a little milk and sprinkle with remaining cheese. Bake at 425°F/220°C/Gas Mark 7 for 25 minutes. Cool and wrap in foil or polythene for freezing.
To serve
Reheat from frozen at 350°F/180°C/Gas Mark 4 for 1 hour.
High Quality Storage Life   2 months

Kedgeree

4 oz/100 g long grain rice
8 oz/200 g cooked smoked haddock fillet
2 oz/50 g unsalted butter
2 teaspoons/10 ml lemon juice
pepper and salt to taste
1 tablespoon chopped fresh parsley

Cook the rice in plenty of fast boiling salted water until *just* tender. Drain and spread out to dry and cool. Free the haddock of all skin and bone, and flake the fish coarsely. When both are quite cold mix the rice and haddock together thoroughly, and add other ingredients.

Use a firm rice which retains its texture, and take care to under rather than overcook it in the first instance. Italian long grain rice gives very good results. Cook the rice in plain salted water, not in the liquid in which the fish was cooked, and use unsalted butter. Hard-boiled egg toughens on freezing, so use a freshly cooked egg for garnishing. Fill into a suitable container, seal, label and freeze.
To serve
Heat gently, breaking up the frozen block with a fork. Cover, and cook over a low heat. Pile onto a hot serving dish and garnish with sliced hard-boiled egg.
High Quality Storage Life   1 month

Fish Rarebit

12 oz/350 g white fish fillet, skinned
salt and pepper
4 oz/100 g coarsely grated Cheddar cheese

Arrange fish in a lightly oiled shallow ovenproof dish. Season. Sprinkle thickly with grated cheese to cover the fish completely. Grill gently until fish is lightly cooked and topping golden. This will take from 5–8 minutes depending on the thickness of the fish. Leave in a cold place to cool quickly. When quite cold cover with foil, label and freeze immediately.
To serve
Uncover, and put into an oven preheated to 400°F/200°C/Gas Mark 6 for 30 minutes.
High Quality Storage Life   1 month

Kedgeree is an excellent dish for a late morning 'brunch'.

Sea pié

Sea Pie

4 oz/100 g short pastry
8 oz/200 g cooked cod or haddock
4 oz/100 g prawns or shrimps
1 oz/25 g butter
1 oz/25 g plain flour
½ pint/250 ml milk
3 oz/75 g grated cheese
2 oz/50 g mushrooms
salt and pepper

Line 9 in/22 cm pie plate or foil dish with pastry and bake blind for 15 minutes. Flake fish and prepare prawns or shrimps if fresh. Melt butter, add flour and cook gently for 1 minute. Stir in milk, and bring to the boil, stirring all the time. Add fish, prawns or shrimps, cheese, mushrooms and seasonings. Cool slightly and pour into pastry case. Bake at 400°F/200°C/Gas Mark 6 for 20 minutes. Cool completely. Pack in polythene or foil.
To serve
Thaw at room temperature for 3 hours to eat cold, or reheat at 325°F/170°C/Gas Mark 3 for 30 minutes to eat hot. Serve garnished with slices of hard-boiled eggs.
High Quality Storage Life   1 month

Potted Crab

4 oz/100 g butter
1 teaspoon black pepper
1 teaspoon ground mace
pinch of Cayenne pepper
8 oz/225 g fresh crabmeat
juice of ½ lemon

Heat ½ oz/15 g butter in a pan, and add pepper, mace and Cayenne pepper. When butter is hot, add crab and lemon juice, and stir well until crab is hot but not brown. Pack into small waxed or plastic cartons. Heat the rest of the butter until it is foamy, skim, and pour over crab, covering it completely. Leave until butter is hard. Pack by covering cartons with lids.
To serve
Thaw overnight in refrigerator, turn out, and serve with hot toast and lemon slices.
High Quality Storage Life   1 month

Hot Kipper Pastries

2 medium kippers
½ oz/15 g butter
¼ pint/125 ml white sauce, (1 oz/25 g butter,
    1 oz/25 g flour, ¼ pint/125 ml milk)
2 oz/50 g grated Cheddar cheese
2 teaspoons/10 ml lemon juice
seasoning
12 oz/350 g short pastry
a little beaten egg or milk

Dot kippers with butter and grill until tender. Skin and fillet. Flake fish and add to white sauce with juices. Add cheese, lemon juice and seasoning. Roll out pastry and cut into four 6 in/15 cm rounds Divide filling between pastry rounds, only covering one half of each round. Brush edges with beaten egg or milk, fold over and seal well. Chill. Brush with beaten egg or milk and bake at 400°F/200°C/ Gas Mark 6 for 30 minutes. Cool, pack and freeze.
To serve
Reheat at 400°F/200°C/Gas Mark 6 for 20 minutes.
High Quality Storage Life   2 months

Fish Puffs

4 oz/100 g plain flour
½ level teaspoon salt
1 tablespoon/15 ml cooking oil
¼ pint/125 ml lukewarm water
8 oz/225 g flaked cooked fish
2 stiffly beaten egg whites
1 tablespoon/15 ml lemon juice
2 level tablespoons chopped capers

Sift together the flour and salt and then mix to a thick batter with the oil and water. Add the fish, lemon juice and capers. Fold in the egg whites. Deep fry dessertspoonsful of the mixture in hot fat or oil at about 375°F/190°C and cook until the puffs are golden brown and crisp. Cool, pack in polythene bag and freeze.
To serve
Thaw for 30 minutes at room temperature, then fry in hot oil or fat until crisp.
High Quality Storage Life   1 month

Salmon or Smoked Haddock Turnovers

8 oz/225 g flaky pastry
8 oz/225 g cooked salmon or smoked haddock
1 oz/25 g butter
1 teaspoon curry powder
salt and pepper
4 tomatoes

Roll pastry into two 12 in/30 cm squares. Flake the fish and mix with melted butter, curry powder, salt and pepper. Divide mixture between two pieces of pastry. Skin tomatoes and cover fish mixture with tomato slices. Fold in corners of pastry to form envelope shapes and seal edges. Pack in foil or polythene bags.
To serve
Put frozen turnovers on tray and bake at 475°F/ 240°C/Gas Mark 9 for 20 minutes, then at 400°F/ 200°C/Gas Mark 6 for 20 minutes.
High Quality Storage Life   1 month

Whitebait

1 lb/450 g frozen whitebait
flour
salt and pepper
pinch of curry powder
sprigs of parsley
lemon wedges

Drain the whitebait well and pat them dry with a paper towel. Put some flour seasoned with salt, pepper and curry powder in a bag and toss the whitebait until they are lightly coated. Heat fat or oil in a deep fryer until smoking. Toss in the whitebait in small quantities and shake them as they cook so they do not stick together. Cook about 3 minutes until golden and crisp. Drain on kitchen paper and keep warm while all the fish are cooked. Plunge the parsley sprigs into the hot fat for 30 seconds until crisp. Garnish the whitebait with parsley and lemon wedges and serve piping hot with thin brown bread and butter.

Halibut in Tomato Sauce

1 tablespoon/15 ml cooking oil
1 large onion
2 oz/50 g olives
2 oz/50 g mushrooms
15 oz/400 g can tomatoes
½ teaspoon mixed herbs
4 halibut steaks

Fry sliced onion, olives and mushrooms in oil for 10 minutes. Add tomatoes, herbs and seasoning and bring to boil. Simmer for 10 minutes. Meanwhile, grill or fry halibut steaks and place in rigid container. Pour sauce over fish, cover, label and freeze.
To serve
Reheat at 300°F/150°C/Gas Mark 2 for 40 minutes.
High Quality Storage Life   2 months

Halibut in tomato sauce is made more exotic when garnished with olives.

Cod with Curry Sauce

1 oz/25 g butter
1 small onion
1 tomato
1 small apple
salt
2 teaspoons curry paste
2 teaspoons/10 ml lemon juice
1 oz/25 g flour
pinch of sugar
$\frac{1}{2}$ pint/250 ml water
1 lb/450 g cod steaks

Fresh or frozen cod steaks may be used for this dish. There is no need to thaw the frozen steaks first. Melt the butter. Chop the onion finely and skin and slice the tomato and apple. Fry the onion, tomato and apple gently until browned lightly. Stir in salt, curry paste, lemon juice, flour and sugar and cook gently for 3 minutes. Stir in water and bring to the boil, stirring well. Add the fish, cover and simmer for 15 minutes. Cool and pack in foil tray, covering the fish with sauce. Cover and freeze.

To serve
Cover tray with a piece of foil and heat at 350°F/180°C/Gas Mark 4 for 40 minutes.
High Quality Storage Life 1 month

Scallops with mushrooms is a delicious starter to any meal.

Scallops with Mushrooms

8 scallops
$\frac{1}{2}$ pint/250 ml dry white wine
1 small onion
parsley, thyme and bay leaf
4 oz/100 g butter
juice of 1 lemon
4 oz/100 g small mushrooms
1 tablespoon plain flour
salt and pepper
2 oz/50 g grated cheese

Clean scallops and put in a pan with wine, chopped onion and herbs. Simmer 5 minutes, no longer as they become tough, and drain scallops, keeping liquid. Melt half the butter, add lemon juice and cook sliced mushrooms until just soft. Drain mushrooms. Add remaining butter to pan, work in flour, and pour in liquid from scallops. Simmer for 2 minutes. Season with salt and pepper and add grated cheese. Cut scallops in pieces, mix with mushrooms and a little sauce, and divide between 8 scallop shells or individual dishes. Coat with remaining sauce. Put shells on to trays, freeze, then wrap in foil.

To serve
Heat frozen scallops at 400°F/200°C/Gas Mark 6 for 20 minutes, after sprinkling surface with a few buttered breadcrumbs which may also be frozen.
High Quality Storage Life   1 month

Fresh trout freezes very well and is delicious baked and grilled served with a herb sauce.

Prawn pizza

Prawn Pizza

Base Dough
8 oz/225 g self-raising flour
½ teaspoon salt
1½ oz/40 g butter
about ¼ pint/125 ml milk
Topping
4 oz/100 g grated Cheddar cheese
1 teaspoon mustard powder
½ teaspoon mixed herbs
8 oz/225 g tomatoes
8 oz/225 g prawns
18 black olives, stoned
paprika

For base dough, sift together flour and salt and rub in butter until mixture is like fine breadcrumbs. Bind with milk to form soft dough. Roll out lightly to 12 in/30 cm circle on greased baking sheet. For topping, mix grated cheese, mustard and herbs in basin. Sprinkle over the dough. Arrange thinly sliced tomatoes on top and then the prawns. Place olives in circle. Sprinkle with paprika. Bake at 400°F/200°C/Gas Mark 6 for 30 minutes. Cool and pack in foil or polythene to freeze.
To serve
Reheat at 400°F/200°C/Gas Mark 6 for 25 minutes.
High Quality Storage Life 1 month

Prawn Quiche

4 oz/100 g short pastry
1 small onion
1 oz butter
6 oz/150 g peeled prawns
salt and black pepper
1 tablespoon chopped parsley
1 egg and 1 egg yolk
5 fl. oz/100 ml single cream
1 oz/25 g Gruyere cheese

Roll out the pastry and line a 6 in/15 cm flan ring. Bake the pastry 'blind' at 425°F/220°C/Gas Mark 7 for 15 minutes, then at 375°F/190°C/Gas Mark 5 for 5 minutes. Grate the onion and fry it gently in butter until yellow. Add the prawns, salt and pepper, and put the mixture into a pastry case. Sprinkle on the parsley. Lightly beat together the eggs, cream and grated cheese, and pour over the prawns. Bake at 350°F/180°C/Gas Mark 4 for 40 minutes until just firm. Wrap and freeze.
To serve
Thaw at room temperature for 3 hours, or reheat in oven.
High Quality Storage Life 1 month

Poultry

Coq Au Vin

2 × 3 lb/1·5 kg chickens
8 oz/225 g bacon
20 small onions
2 oz/50 g butter
2 fl. oz/50 ml oil
2 tablespoons/30 ml brandy
salt and pepper
1 tablespoon/15 ml tomato purée
1 pint/500 ml red wine
sprig of parsley
sprig of thyme
1 bay leaf
pinch of ground nutmeg
1 garlic clove
12 oz/350 g button mushrooms
1 oz/25 g butter
$\frac{1}{2}$ oz/15 g cornflour

Chicken joints may be used for this dish if preferred, but otherwise the chickens should be cut into joints. Cut the bacon in strips and simmer in a little water for 10 minutes. Drain well. Peel the onions. Heat the butter and oil together and fry the bacon lightly until brown. Remove from the pan and brown the onions in the fat. Remove the onions and cook the chicken joints for about 10 minutes until golden on all sides. Add the bacon and onions, cover and cook over low heat for 10 minutes. Pour on the brandy and ignite it, rotating the pan until the flame dies out. Season with salt and pepper, and add the tomato purée, wine, herbs, nutmeg and crushed garlics. Cover and simmer for 1 hour. Remove the chicken piece and put into a freezer container.

Cook the mushrooms in butter until just tender and add to the chicken pieces. Stir the cornflour into a little water and add to the cooking liquid. Simmer until smooth and creamy. Cool and pour over the chicken and mushrooms. Cover and freeze.

To serve
Transfer the dish to an ovenware container, cover and heat at 400°F/200°C/Gas Mark 6 for 45 minutes. Garnish with parsley and triangles of fried bread.
High Quality Storage Life   2 months

Chicken in Tomato Sauce

2 lb/1 kg cooked chicken meat
14 oz/400 g canned tomatoes
1 garlic clove
1 medium onion
1 green pepper
4 tablespoons/60 ml olive oil
1 teaspoon basil
$\frac{1}{2}$ teaspoon marjoram
1 tablespoon/15 ml tomato purée
salt and pepper
1 tablespoon/15 ml white wine
6 drops Tabasco sauce

Cut the chicken into neat pieces. Put the tomatoes and juice through a sieve. Crush the garlic and chop the onion and pepper finely. Cook the garlic, onion and pepper in hot oil until just soft. Stir in tomatoes, herbs, tomato purée, salt, pepper, wine and Tabasco sauce. Simmer for 15 minutes. Stir in the chicken and cook for 5 minutes. Pack into a foil container when cool, and cover with a lid for freezer storage.
To serve
Replace lid with foil and heat at 350°F/180°C/Gas Mark 4 for 1 hour. Sprinkle with chopped parsley before serving.
High Quality Storage Life   4 months

Coq au vin is a classic French dish made from chicken pieces with bacon and mushrooms

Chicken Patties

8 oz/225 g cooked chicken
4 oz/100 g fresh white breadcrumbs
2 teaspoons/10 ml Worcestershire sauce
salt and pepper
2 eggs
a few dry breadcrumbs

Mince the chicken finely. Mix with the breadcrumbs, sauce, salt and pepper and beaten eggs. If necessary, add a little leftover gravy to bind the mixture. Shape into eight flat cakes and dust with dry breadcrumbs. Open-freeze and then pack in polythene for storage.
To serve
Fry from frozen in hot oil until golden on both sides and cooked through. Serve hot or cold.
High Quality Storage Life   2 months

Country Chicken Pie

4 lb/2 kg chicken
3 rashers streaky bacon
1 tablespoon chopped parsley
pinch of mixed herbs
salt and pepper
12 oz/350 g shortcrust pastry

Remove the giblets from the bird. Put the chicken into a pan with all the giblets except the liver (save that for an omelette or pâté) and just cover with water. Bring to the boil, then reduce heat and simmer for 1½ hours. Cool and remove the chicken meat from the bones. Arrange the chicken meat in layers in a pie-dish which will go in the freezer, along with chopped bacon, parsley and herbs. Season each layer lightly with salt and pepper. Thicken the chicken stock with a little cornflour and cover the chicken. Cool completely and cover with the pastry. Bake at 450°F/230°C/Gas Mark 8 for 45 minutes. Cool and pack into a polythene bag to freeze.

Country chicken pie

To serve
Reheat at 350°F/180°C/Gas Mark 4 for 1 hour, covering the pastry if it becomes too brown. The pie may be frozen with uncooked pastry, and should then be baked straight from the freezer at 450°F/230°C/Gas Mark 8 for 45 minutes, then at 375°F/190°C/Gas Mark 5 for 20 minutes.
High Quality Storage Life   2 months

Farmhouse Chicken

4 chicken portions
seasoned flour
1 oz/25 g butter
2 tablespoons/30 ml oil
2 onions
2 carrots
1 green pepper
$\frac{3}{4}$ pint/375 ml chicken stock
pinch of tarragon

Coat the chicken portions with the flour. Melt the butter and oil together and fry the chicken quickly until golden on all sides. Transfer to a casserole. Chop the onions, slice the carrots and green pepper. Cook these in the fat until soft and golden, and add to the chicken. Pour in the stock and add the tarragon. Cover and cook at 350°F/180°C/Gas Mark 4 for 1$\frac{1}{4}$ hours. Cool, pack in a foil container, cover and freeze.
To serve
Reheat at 325°F/170°C/Gas Mark 3 for 1 hour and stir in $\frac{1}{4}$ pint/125 ml single cream just before serving.
High Quality Storage Life   2 months

Duck with orange is a famous French dish, ideally suited to freezing.

Duck with Orange

4 oz/100 g streaky bacon
1 medium onion
1 carrot
3 tablespoons/40 g plain flour
3 teaspoons tomato purée
¾ pint/375 ml stock
4 tablespoons/60 ml sherry
1 duck
3 oz/75 g butter
juice of 2 oranges
salt and pepper
1 orange

Cut the bacon in small pieces and put over gentle heat to extract fat. Remove bacon pieces, and add sliced onion and carrot to the fat. Cook over low heat till lightly browned. Stir in flour and cook till brown, then add tomato purée. Pour on the stock slowly, and stir in sherry. Cook very gently till mushrooms are tender, then strain in this sauce. Put the duck into casserole. Pour on sauce, and the juice of two oranges. Season well, cover, and cook at 350°F/180°C/Gas Mark 4 for 1 hour. Remove the orange skins, and cut into fine slices. Add to casserole 15 minutes before the end of cooking. Cool, pack into rigid container and freeze.
To serve
Reheat at 325°F/170°C/Gas Mark 3 for 1 hour.
High Quality Storage Life   2 months

Meat Dishes

Pork Carbonnade

1½ lb/675 g shoulder pork
2 leeks
1 garlic clove
1 oz/25 g lard
2 oz/50 g plain flour
salt and pepper
½ pint/250 ml brown ale
sprig of parsley
sprig of thyme
1 bayleaf
few drops of Tabasco sauce
piece of lemon peel
3 oz/75 g button mushrooms

Cut the pork into cubes. Chop the leeks and crush the garlic. Fry the leeks and garlic in lard until soft and golden. Toss the pork in seasoned flour and add to leeks. Fry for 5 minutes. Add the remaining ingredients and bring to the boil. Cover and simmer for 1¼ hours. Cool and pack into a foil container with lid to freeze.
To serve
Replace lid with foil and reheat at 350°F/180°C/Gas Mark 4 for 1 hour.
High Quality Storage Life 2 months

Little Meat Balls

12 oz/350 g minced fresh beef
4 oz/100 g minced fresh pork
2 oz/50 g dry white breadcrumbs
½ pint/250 ml creamy milk
1 small onion
1 oz/25 g butter
salt and pepper

Mix together the beef and pork. Soak the breadcrumbs in the milk. Chop the onion finely and cook in the butter until soft and golden. Mix the bread-crumbs and onion with the meat and season well. The mixture will be soft. Shape into small balls and fry a few at a time in butter until evenly browned, shaking the pan to keep the meatballs round. Drain each batch and cool. Pack in bags or rigid containers to freeze.
To serve
Thaw in wrappings in refrigerator for 3 hours to eat cold with salad. To serve hot, fry quickly in hot fat, or heat in gravy or tomato sauce.
High Quality Storage Life 2 months

Goulash

2 lb/1 kg chuck steak
2 tablespoons bacon fat
6 medium onions
2 tablespoons/30 g paprika
½ teaspoon/8 g salt
2 green peppers

Pork may be used instead of beef. Cut the meat into cubes. Put half the meat into a pan and cook in its own fat until lightly browned. Put the meat into a saucepan. Rinse out the frying pan with ½ pint/250 ml water and add this water to the meat. Repeat the process with the remaining meat. Melt the fat and cook the coarsely chopped onions until soft and golden. Stir in the paprika and salt, and add to the meat with the chopped green peppers. Cover and simmer for about 2 hours until the meat is tender. Cool, pack in a rigid container, cover and freeze.
To serve
Reheat gently and serve with noodles or plain boiled potatoes. Some soured cream or yogurt may be stirred into the goulash just before serving.
High Quality Storage Life 2 months

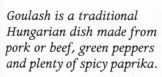

Goulash is a traditional Hungarian dish made from pork or beef, green peppers and plenty of spicy paprika.

Beef in Beer

2 lb/1 kg lean topside
1 oz/25 g plain flour
salt and pepper
3 medium onions
¾ pint/375 ml brown stock
½ pint/250 ml mild ale
½ oz/15 g caster sugar
pinch of mixed herbs
1 oz/25 g dripping

Cut the meat into four slices. Season the flour and coat the meat in it. Melt the dripping and seal the meat on both sides. Slice the onions and cook until soft and golden. Put the meat and onions into a casserole and add the remaining ingredients. Cover and simmer at 350°F/180°C/Gas Mark 4 for 1½ hours. Cool and remove surplus fat. Pack into a foil container and cover with a lid to freeze.
To serve
Replace lid with foil and reheat at 350°F/180°C/Gas Mark 4 for 1 hour.
High Quality Storage Life   4 months

Spiced Beef Casserole

2 lb/1 kg chuck or brisket beef
2 oz/50 g butter
2 large onions
1 garlic clove
½ pint/250 ml stock or water
¼ pint/125 ml red wine
12 oz/350 g carrots
2 teaspoons/10 ml tomato purée
1 bay leaf
sprig of parsley
sprig of thyme
¼ teaspoon ground mace
½ teaspoon caraway seeds
salt and pepper
8 oz/225 g large mushrooms
1 tablespoon/15 g cornflour

Cut the meat into cubes and remove excess fat. Melt the butter and brown the meat all over. Add the sliced onions and crushed garlic and continue cooking for 5 minutes. Add the stock, wine, sliced carrots, tomato purée, herbs, spices and seasoning. Cover and simmer for 1 hour. Add the thickly sliced mushrooms and continue cooking for 30 minutes. Take out the herbs. Mix the cornflour with a little water and stir into the pan. Bring to the boil, and stir for a few minutes until the gravy is smooth and creamy. Cool and pack into a foil container, covering with a lid to freeze.

To serve
Replace lid with foil and reheat at 350°F/180°C/Gas Mark 4 for 1 hour.
High Quality Storage Life   4 months

Lamb and Lentil Bake

1½ lb/750 g middle and scrag end of lamb
2 onions
4 oz/100 g lentils (soaked overnight)
15 oz/425 g canned tomatoes
½ pint/250 ml stock
salt and pepper

Cut the lamb in pieces and brown in its own fat. Lift out the lamb pieces into a casserole. Slice the onions and cook in the remaining fat until soft and golden. Add to the lamb with the drained lentils, tomatoes in their juice, stock, salt and pepper. Cover and cook at 350°F/180°C/Gas Mark 4 for 1¼ hours. Cool and pack in rigid or foil container to freeze.
To serve
Reheat at 350°F/180°C/Gas Mark 4 for 1 hour and sprinkle with chopped fresh parsley before serving.
High Quality Storage Life   2 months

Stuffed cabbage rolls are prepared with a filling of meat and rice and may be served with gravy or with a tomato sauce.

Stuffed Cabbage Rolls

1 lb/450 g minced cold meat
1 oz/25 g butter
1 small onion
2 tablespoons/25 g cooked rice
1 teaspoon chopped parsley
salt and pepper
stock
12 medium-sized cabbage leaves

Cook the meat in the butter with the finely chopped onion until the meat begins to colour. Mix with rice, parsley, salt, pepper and enough stock to moisten, and cook for 5 minutes. Blanch cabbage leaves in boiling water for 2 minutes and drain well. Put a spoonful of filling on each leaf, and form into a parcel. Put parcels close together in a covered oven dish and cover with stock. Cook at 350°F/180°C/ Gas Mark 4 for 45 minutes, and then cool. Put into a foil container, cover and freeze.
To serve
Remove lid and reheat at 350°F/180°C/Gas Mark 4 for 1 hour with a covering of foil so that the cabbage leaves remain soft. If liked, thicken the cooking liquid with a small ball of butter and flour worked together and stirred in about 5 minutes before serving time.
High Quality Storage Life 2 months

Steak and kidney pie may be made with shortcrust or puff pastry and mushrooms or onions may be added for extra flavouring.

Steak and Kidney Pie

1 lb/450 g chuck steak
4 oz/100 g ox kidney
1 oz/25 g dripping
¾ pint/375 ml beef stock
salt and pepper
½ oz/15 g cornflour
8 oz/225 g puff pastry

Cut the steak and kidney into neat pieces and fry until brown in the dripping. Add stock and seasoning and simmer for 2 hours. Mix the cornflour with a little water. Stir into the hot mixture, and simmer for a few minutes until the gravy is smooth and creamy. Pour into a foil dish, or into a pie dish which will withstand freezer temperatures. Cool the meat, cover with pastry, pack into a polythene bag and freeze.
To serve
Unwrap and bake at 400°F/200°C/Gas Mark 6 for 50 minutes until pastry is crisp and golden.
High Quality Storage Life 2 months

OVERLEAF: *A mixed grill of lamb chops, bacon, sausages and liver is always a welcome treat, served with onions mushrooms and tomatoes.*

Pork casserole made with root vegetables and potatoes may be accompanied by more potatoes or pasta or rice to make a really nourishing meal.

Pork Casserole

2 lb/1 kg lean pork
2 large onions
8 oz/225 g carrots
2 oz/50 g lard
2 pints/1 litre stock
salt and pepper
2 lb/1 kg potatoes
chopped parsley

Cut the pork into cubes. Slice the onions and carrots. Melt the lard and cook the pork until light brown. Remove from fat and put into a casserole. Cook the onions and carrots in the fat until golden and add to the pork. Cover with the stock and season well. Cover and cook at 350°F/180°C/Gas Mark 4 for 1½ hours. Cut the potatoes into large chunks, add to the pork and continue cooking for 30 minutes. For immediate use, serve garnished with chopped parsley. To freeze, cool, and pack into a rigid container.

To serve

Return to casserole, cover and heat at 350°F/180°C/ Gas Mark 4 for 50 minutes. If preferred, the casserole may be frozen after only 1½ hours' cooking, without the potatoes. It can then be reheated for 50 minutes, potatoes added and cooking continued for 30 minutes. This is particularly worthwhile in the early summer, as small whole new potatoes can be used.

High Quality Storage Life   2 months

124

Winter Lamb Stew

2 oz/50 g butter
8 middle neck lamb chops
8 oz/225 g onions
8 oz/225 g leeks
12 oz/350 g carrots
4 oz/100 g turnips
1¼ pints/625 ml stock or water
¼ teaspoon rosemary
½ teaspoon grated lemon rind
salt and pepper
1 tablespoon/15 g cornflour

Melt the butter and fry the chop gently for 1 minute on each side. Add sliced onions, leeks and carrots, and diced turnips. Fry gently for 5 minutes, turning occasionally. Add stock, rosemary, lemon rind and seasoning. Bring to the boil, cover and simmer gently for 1¼ hours. Mix the cornflour with a little cold water. Remove stew from heat, add cornflour and stir well. Return to the heat, bring to the boil, and cook for 5 minutes, stirring well. Cool and pack into a foil container, covering with a lid to freeze.
To serve
Remove lid and cover with foil and reheat at 350°F/180°C/Gas Mark 4 for 1 hour. If liked, a few frozen peas may be stirred into the stew during reheating.
High Quality Storage Life 4 months

Sweet and Sour Lamb

1½ lb/675 g boned breast of lamb
1 medium onion
1 medium carrot
½ pint/250 ml stock
1 tablespoon vinegar
2 teaspoons/10 g cornflour
2 teaspoons/10 ml soy sauce
2 teaspoons/10 g brown sugar

Cut the meat into thin strips and fry in its own fat until crisp. Drain off fat. Slice the onion and carrot and add to the lamb with the stock. Add the vinegar, cornflour blended with a little water, soy sauce and sugar. Cover and simmer for 1 hour. Cool and pack into a polythene bag to freeze.
To serve
Reheat gently in a double saucepan and serve with rice or noodles.
High Quality Storage Life 2 months

Veal with Olives

1 lb/450 g pie veal
3 tablespoons/45 ml olive oil
2 onions
2 tablespoons flour
½ glass white wine
½ pint/250 ml stock
4 oz/100 g mushrooms
2 tablespoons/30 ml tomato purée
1 garlic clove
12 pitted green olives
pepper

Cut veal in pieces and fry till golden in oil. Slice onions and fry till golden. Sprinkle in flour, and cook till brown. Stir in wine and stock, bring to boil, and add sliced mushrooms, tomato purée and crushed garlic. Cover and cook at 325°F/170°C/Gas Mark 3 for 1 hour. Add olives and a good shake of pepper 5 minutes before cooking finishes. Cool, pack in rigid container and freeze.
To serve
Reheat at 325°F/170°C/Gas Mark 3 for 1 hour.
High Quality Storage Life 2 months

Breast of Lamb Casserole

3 lb/1½ kg breast of lamb
1 large onion
2 garlic cloves
4 tablespoons/60 ml vinegar
1 tablespoon/15 ml Worcestershire sauce
1½ teaspoons salt
1½ teaspoons chilli powder
pinch of Cayenne pepper
¼ teaspoon pepper
¼ pint/125 ml bottled sauce
¼ pint/125 ml water

Cut lamb in serving pieces, trimming off surplus fat. Brown slightly on all sides. Pour off fat, and put meat into casserole. Mix all other ingredients, and pour over meat. Cover and bake at 350°F/180°C/Gas Mark 4 for 1¼ hours. Cool, pack in rigid container and freeze.
To serve
Reheat at 325°F/170°C/Gas Mark 3 for 45 minutes. Take off cover and bake for 15 minutes.
High Quality Storage Life 2 months

Breast of Veal with Sausage Stuffing

3 lb/1½ kg boned breast of veal
8 oz/225 g pork sausage meat
salt and pepper
¼ pint/125 ml water
4 tablespoons/60 ml bottled sauce
1 onion

Spread the veal with the sausage meat, roll it up, and tie it securely. Sprinkle the meat with salt and pepper and brown it all over in a little hot fat. Add the water, sauce and sliced onion, cover and simmer for 2 hours. Cool and remove surplus fat. Pack in rigid container to freeze.
To serve
Reheat at 350°F/180°C/Gas Mark 4 for 1 hour.
High Quality Storage Life   1 month

Breast of veal can be stuffed with sausage meat for a rich entrée.

Soak beans in water overnight. Heat the oil in pan and fry the onion and chopped bacon for 3 minutes. Add the cubed pork and fry for 5 minutes, turning meat. Drain the butter beans and add with the cubed garlic sausage, stock, tomatoes with juice, herbs and seasoning. Bring to the boil, stirring. Transfer to a large foil container, cover and bake at 325°F/170°C/Gas Mark 3 for 1½ hours. Remove the herbs, sprinkle the top with breadcrumbs and bake, uncovered, for 30 minutes. Cool, cover and freeze.
To serve
Uncover and reheat at 350°F/180°C/Gas Mark 4 for 1 hour.
High Quality Storage Life   2 months

Brown Veal Casserole

1½ lb/675 g stewing veal
3 rashers bacon
2 carrots
2 onions
1 stick celery
2 oz/50 g butter
2 oz/50 g flour
1 pint/500 ml water
1 dessertspoon/10 ml tomato purée
2 teaspoons/10 ml Worcestershire sauce
1 teaspoon/5 ml meat extract
salt and pepper
2 sprigs parsley
2 strips lemon peel
1 tablespoon/15 ml dry sherry

Cut veal in cubes, bacon and carrots in narrow strips, and slice the onions finely. Cut the celery in small chunks. Melt butter, lightly colour the vegetables, and remove to casserole. Sprinkle the flour into the remaining butter, cook till brown, then gradually add the water and stir till the sauce thickens. Add tomato purée, Worcestershire sauce, meat extract, parsley, salt and pepper, and the lemon peel from which the white pith has been removed. Bring to boil, then add sherry. Put the meat in the casserole with the vegetables, pour over the sauce, mix well, and cover tightly. Cook in a slow oven, 300°F/160°C/Gas Mark 2 for 2 hours. Cool, pack in rigid container and freeze.
Reheat at 325°F/170°C/Gas Mark 3 for 45 minutes.
High Quality Storage Life   2 months

Cassoulet

8 oz/225 g dried butter beans
1 tablespoon/15 ml cooking oil
1 large onion, chopped
4 oz/100 g streaky bacon
2 lb/1 kg belly pork
8 oz/225 g garlic sausage
1¼ pints/625 ml stock
8 oz/225 g canned tomatoes
½ oz/15 g parsley and thyme and 1 bay leaf
salt and pepper
4 oz/100 g fresh breadcrumbs

LEFT: *Kidneys in red wine make a tasty supper dish or may be served with vegetables or on toast.*

Lamb Cutlets

Kidneys in Red Wine

10 lamb's kidneys
1 small onion
4 oz/100 g small button mushrooms
1½ oz/40 g butter
1 garlic clove
½ oz/15 g plain flour
¼ pint/125 ml red wine
4 tablespoons/60 ml beef stock
salt and pepper
1 teaspoon made mustard

Skin the kidneys and cut them in half, carefully taking out the hard white core. Chop the onion finely and slice the mushrooms. Melt the butter and cook the kidneys for 3 minutes. Remove them and put into a small pan. Cook the onion, crushed garlic and mushrooms in the fat for 2 minutes and stir in the flour. Pour in the wine and stock and bring to the boil. Add the kidneys and season with salt, pepper and mustard. Simmer for 10 minutes. Cool and pack in a rigid container to freeze.
To serve
Reheat gently until piping hot and serve garnished with chopped parsley.
High Quality Storage Life 2 months

Cumberland Cutlets

8 best end neck lamb cutlets
oil
1 small onion
1 garlic clove
4 oz/100 g mushrooms
1 red pepper
1 tablespoon/15 ml tomato purée
¼ pint/125 ml stock
1 tablespoon/125 ml lemon juice
2 teaspoons sugar
salt and pepper

Fry the cutlets in hot oil until brown on both sides. Remove from the pan and place in a casserole. Fry the chopped onion and garlic until soft and the sliced mushrooms until lightly browned. Drain and place in the casserole with the cutlets. Add the sliced red pepper. Mix together the tomato purée, stock and lemon juice and pour into the casserole. Season with sugar, salt and pepper. Cover and bake at 350°F/180°C/Gas Mark 4 for 45 minutes. Allow to cool. Put chops and sauce in foil container, seal, label and freeze.
To serve
Reheat at 375°F/190°C/Gas Mark 5 for 45 minutes.
High Quality Storage Life 1 month

Savoury Dishes, Pastries and Pasta

Lincolnshire Haslet

2 lb/1 kg lean pork
1 small onion
8 oz/225 g stale bread
½ oz/15 g salt
1 teaspoon pepper
1 teaspoon sage

Mince the meat and onion coarsely. Cut the bread into cubes and soak in a little water. Squeeze out the moisture and mix the bread with the meat. Season with the salt, pepper and finely chopped sage. Put into a loaf tin and bake at 350°F/180°C/Gas Mark 4 for 1 hour. Cool in the tin and turn out. Wrap in foil or polythene to freeze.
To serve
Thaw at room temperature for 3 hours and serve in slices with salad.
High Quality Storage Life 2 months

Liver Loaf

8 oz/225 g liver
2 oz/50 g streaky bacon
4 oz/100 g pork sausage meat
1 medium onion
2 oz/50 g fresh white breadcrumbs
1 teaspoon/5 ml Worcestershire sauce
1 egg
salt and pepper
pinch of mixed herbs
¼ pint/125 ml water

Slice the liver and fry lightly in a little butter or bacon fat. Put through a coarse mincer with the bacon and onion. Mix with the sausage meat, bread-crumbs, sauce, egg, salt, pepper and herbs and add enough of the water to make a soft mixture. Put into a greased loaf tin and cover with a lid or foil. Bake at 400°F/200°C/Gas Mark 6 for 45 minutes. Cool in the tin and turn out. Wrap in foil or polythene to freeze.
To serve
Thaw at room temperature for 3 hours and carve in slices with salad.
High Quality Storage Life 2 months

Quick Mushroom Pizza

12 oz/350 g self-raising flour
1 teaspoon salt
¼ pint/125 ml cooking oil
6 tablespoons/90 ml water
1 lb/450 g mushrooms
6 oz/150 g onions
6 oz/150 g lean bacon
pepper
pinch of rosemary
4 oz/100 g Gruyère cheese
1 oz/25 g Parmesan cheese

Mix the flour and salt and mix with the oil and water to make a soft dough. Divide into 2 pieces and roll to make a soft dough. Divide into 2 pieces and roll out into large thin rounds. Bake at 450°F/220°C/Gas Mark 8 for 15 minutes and cool. Chop the mushrooms. Chop the onions and bacon. Put the bacon into a pan and heat gently until the fat runs. Stir in the onions and continue cooking until the onions are soft and golden. Add the mushrooms and cook until they are just soft. Season with pepper and rosemary and spread the mixture on the two baked circles. Top with a thick crust of grated cheese. Wrap in foil or polythene to freeze.
To serve
Unwrap and cover loosely with foil. Bake from frozen at 350°F/180°C/Gas Mark 4 for 45 minutes. Remove foil and continue heating for 10 minutes.
High Quality Storage Life 1 month

Quick mushroom pizza is made from scone dough with a savoury filling and a thick topping of grated cheese.

130

Savoury Lamb Pie

1 lb/450 g fillet of neck of lamb
2 large onions
3 lambs' kidneys
1 teaspoon sage
4 oz/100 g button mushrooms
½ pint/250 ml stock
salt and pepper
a little flour
Pastry
4 oz/100 g plain flour
2 oz/50 g margarine
1 oz/25 g Cheddar cheese
beaten egg to glaze

Ask the butcher to cut the fillet from the neck of lamb, and then cut the meat into 1 in/2·5 cm cubes. Fry the lamb in its own fat. Add the chopped onions, chopped kidneys, sage, stock and seasoning. Bring to the boil, cover and simmer for 1 hour. Add the mushrooms and then thicken the liquid with a little flour if a thick sauce is liked. Put into a freezer-proof pie dish or foil container. Make the pastry with the flour, fat and grated cheese and mix with a little cold water to a stiff dough. Roll out the pastry and cover the pie. Brush with beaten egg and bake at 400°F/200°C/Gas Mark 6 for 30 minutes. Cool, pack in polythene bag and freeze.
To serve
Reheat at 350°F/180°C/Gas Mark 4 for 50 minutes.
High Quality Storage Life 2 months

Spaghetti Bolognese

2 tablespoons/30 ml oil
2 oz/50 g onions
1 lb/450 g raw minced beef
14 oz/350 g canned tomatoes
2 oz/50 g concentrated tomato purée
½ pint/250 ml beef stock
pinch of marjoram
1 bay leaf
1 lb/450 g spaghetti

Heat the oil and fry the chopped onions and beef until golden. Add the tomatoes with the juice, purée, stock and herbs, with salt and pepper to taste. Simmer for at least 45 minutes, stirring occasionally. If liked, use a little red wine in place of some of the stock. A chopped chicken liver and a crushed garlic clove give added richness and flavour to the sauce. Remove the bayleaf before freezing the dish. While the sauce is cooking, cook the spaghetti in a large pan of boiling salted water for about 12 minutes until tender but still firm. Drain the spaghetti very well and put in the middle of a large foil container. Put the sauce round the spaghetti, cover and freeze. The pasta in composite dishes should be placed in the middle of the container as it heats more quickly than the sauce and can dry out when reheated. The sauce can be packed separately in a rigid container for freezing, to be paired with freshly-cooked pasta.
To serve
Remove lid and cover the container with foil. Heat at 375°F/190°C/Gas Mark 5 for 45 minutes. If the sauce is frozen separately, reheat it gently in a double saucepan.
High Quality Storage Life 2 months

Spaghetti Bolognese may be frozen as a complete dish or the sauce and pasta can be frozen separately.

Fish Pudding

1 lb/450 g haddock
3 oz/75 g shredded suet
3 oz/75 g breadcrumbs
2 teaspoons chopped parsley
1 teaspoon chopped onion
2 eggs
½ pint/250 ml milk
salt and pepper

The fish should not be cooked for this dish, but may be fresh or thawed frozen fish. Remove any skin and bone and chop the flesh finely. Mix with the suet, breadcrumbs, parsley, onion, beaten eggs and milk. Season well with salt and pepper. Put into a well-greased foil pudding basin, cover with greased paper and foil, and steam the pudding for 1 hour.

Cool and pack in polythene to freeze.
To serve
Put the basin with a covering of foil into a pan of boiling water and steam for 45 minutes. Turn out and serve with parsley, tomato or mushroom sauce.
High Quality Storage Life   2 months

Normandy Rabbit

1 young rabbit
3 oz/75 g butter
4 garlic cloves
1 tablespoon/15 ml concentrated tomato purée
½ pint/250 ml cider
salt and pepper

Soak the rabbit joints in cold water for 30 minutes and drain. Cover with fresh cold water and simmer for 30 minutes. Drain well and remove meat from bones in large neat pieces. Fry the rabbit in the butter with the crushed garlic cloves until just golden. Stir in the tomato purée and add the cider and seasoning. Simmer for 10 minutes and cool. Pack into a rigid container, making sure the rabbit pieces are covered with sauce.
To serve
Reheat gently on low heat, or in a low oven, and serve garnished with plenty of chopped parsley.
High Quality Storage Life   2 months

Cheese Loaf

3 oz/75 g soft margarine
8 oz/225 g self-raising flour
1 teaspoon baking powder
1 teaspoon mustard powder
½ teaspoon salt
¼ teaspoon pepper
4 bacon rashers
1 egg
3 oz/75 g Cheddar cheese
¼ pint/125 ml milk

Put the margarine into a bowl with the flour, baking powder, mustard, salt and pepper. Chop the bacon and add to the bowl with the egg and cheese. Pour in the milk and beat together with a wooden spoon until well mixed. Put into a 1 lb/450 g loaf tin, lined on the bottom with greaseproof paper. Bake at 375°F/190°C/Gas Mark 5 for 45 minutes. Leave in the tin for 5 minutes, then turn out and cool on a wire rack. Pack in foil or polythene to freeze.
To serve
Thaw at room temperature for 3 hours and serve with salad or soup.
High Quality Storage Life   2 months

133

Macaroni Cheese

8 oz/225 g macaroni
2 oz/50 g butter
2 oz/50 g plain flour
1½ pints/750 ml milk
8 oz/225 g Cheddar cheese
salt and pepper

Cook the macaroni as directed on the packet and drain well. Melt the butter and work in the flour. Cook for 1 minute and work in the milk. Stir over gentle heat until the sauce is smooth and creamy. Over very low heat, stir in the grated cheese and seasoning. Mix the macaroni and cheese sauce and cool. Pack into a foil container and cover with a lid to freeze. If liked, some chopped cooked ham or bacon, chopped cooked onions, or mushrooms can be added to the macaroni cheese before freezing.
To serve
Cover with foil and heat at 400°F/200°C/Gas Mark 6 for 1 hour, removing the foil for the last 15 minutes to brown the top.
High Quality Storage Life   2 months

Quiche Lorraine

8 oz/225 g shortcrust pastry
½ oz/15 g butter
1 small onion
1 oz/25 g streaky bacon
1 egg
1 egg yolk
2 oz/50 g grated Cheddar cheese
¼ pint/125 ml creamy milk
pepper

Line a 7 in/17·5 cm flan ring with pastry, or line a foil dish which can be put into the freezer. Melt the butter and cook the chopped onion and bacon until golden. Put into the pastry case. Lightly beat together the egg, egg yolk, cheese and milk. Season with pepper and a little salt, if the bacon is not very salty. Pour into the pastry case. Bake at 375°F/190°C/Gas Mark 5 for 30 minutes. Cool. Cover a foil container with polythene, or pack in a rigid container to prevent breakage.
To serve
Thaw in refrigerator for 6 hours to serve cold. If preferred hot, heat at 350°F/180°C/Gas Mark 4 for 20 minutes.
High Quality Storage Life   2 months

Quiche Lorraine may be served hot or cold and is a tasty addition to a picnic tea.

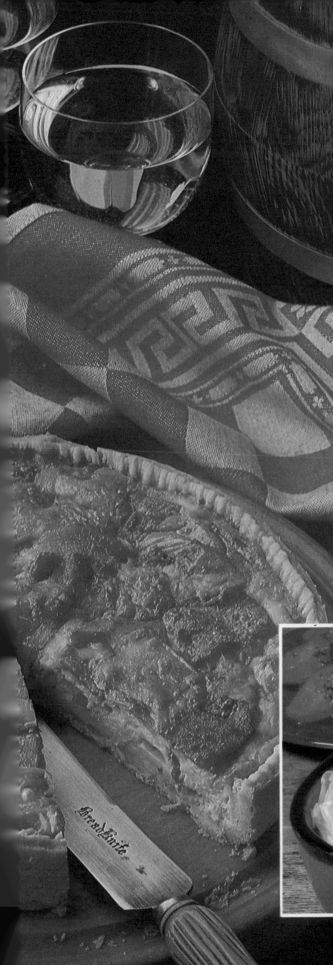

Spinach Noodles with Cheese

1 lb/450 g noodles
½ oz/15 g butter
1 large onion
1 garlic clove
8 oz/225 g lean bacon
1 lb/450 g spinach
½ pint/250 ml soured cream
salt and pepper
pinch of nutmeg
7 oz/200 g Gruyère cheese

Cook the noodles in boiling water from 6–8 minutes until tender and drain thoroughly. Chop the onion finely and crush the garlic clove and cook in the butter until soft and golden. Chop the bacon and cook with the onions until soft. Stir the onion and bacon into the noodles and arrange in a freezer-to-table container. Wash the spinach very well and put into a saucepan without any water. Cook over gentle heat until the spinach is soft. Drain very thoroughly and press out any liquid. Mash the spinach with a potato masher and then work in the soured cream, salt, pepper and nutmeg. Arrange in the centre of the noodles. Cool completely and cover with thin slices of cheese. Cover with foil or a lid to freeze.

To serve
Remove lid and cover dish with foil. Heat at 350°F/180°C/Gas Mark 4 for 40 minutes. Remove foil and continue cooking for 15 minutes until the cheese has melted.

High Quality Storage Life   1 month

Noodles with spinach makes a delicious light meal for lunch or supper, accompanied by a fresh salad.

135

Fresh chicory, in season, is now readily available in most greengrocers. It is simple to prepare, and is delicious cooked in cheese.

Chicory with Cheese

4 chicory heads
4 slices cooked ham
1 oz/25 g butter
4 slices Cheddar cheese
1 oz/25 g breadcrumbs

Cook the chicory in a little stock, or in some water with lemon juice for 25 minutes. Drain well and wrap each chicory head in a piece of ham. Butter a foil freezer container and put in the chicory and ham. Cover with cheese and sprinkle with the breadcrumbs and flakes of butter. Bake at 375°F/190°C/Gas Mark 5 for 15 minutes. Cool, cover and freeze.
To serve
Uncover and reheat at 350°F/180°C/Gas Mark 4 for 30 minutes.
High Quality Storage Life 1 month

Bacon Pasties

12 oz/350 g shortcrust pastry
6 oz/150 g streaky bacon
4 oz/100 g lamb's kidneys
1 large onion
8 oz/225 g raw minced beef
salt and pepper
½ teaspoon Worcestershire sauce

Roll out pastry and cut six 7 in/17·5 cm rounds. Chop the bacon, kidneys and onion finely and mix with the minced beef. Season well with salt, pepper and Worcestershire sauce. Put a spoonful of mixture on each pastry round and form into pasty shapes, sealing the edges well. Put on a wet baking sheet and bake at 425°F/220°C/Gas Mark 7 for 45 minutes. Cool and pack in polythene to freeze.
To serve
Thaw for 2 hours at room temperature.
High Quality Storage Life 1 month

Cornish Fish Pasties

8 oz/225 g smoked haddock fillets
1 oz/25 g butter
1 oz/25 g plain flour
½ pint/250 ml milk
2 tablespoons finely chopped parsley
1 teaspoon mustard powder
12 oz/350 g shortcrust pastry
beaten egg for glazing

Cook the haddock and remove any skin and bones. Flake the flesh. Melt the butter, stir in the flour and cook for 1 minute. Add the milk and stir over low heat until thick and creamy. Remove from the heat and add the parsley and mustard, and then stir in the fish. Leave until cool. Roll out the pastry and cut out five 6 in/15 cm circles, using a saucer as a guide. Put a spoonful of the fish mixture in the centre of each, dampen the edges and form into pasties. Brush with beaten egg and bake at 375°F/190°C/Gas Mark 5 for 30 minutes. Cool and pack in polythene to freeze.

To serve
Reheat from frozen at 350°F/180°C/Gas Mark 4 for 30 minutes.
High Quality Storage Life   2 months

Fish Pie

8 oz/225 g cooked halibut
3 tomatoes
4 oz/100 g button mushrooms
juice of $\frac{1}{2}$ lemon
1 tablespoon chopped parsley
1 oz/25 g butter
1 oz/25 g plain flour
$\frac{1}{2}$ pint/250 milk
salt and pepper
pinch of ground nutmeg
12 oz/350 g puff pastry
beaten egg to glaze

Cut the fish into pieces and arrange in layers with sliced tomatoes and mushrooms in a freezer-proof pie dish or foil container, sprinkling the layers with lemon juice and parsley. Melt the butter and stir in the flour. Cook for 1 minute and blend in the milk. Stir over gentle heat until the sauce thickens. Season with salt, pepper and nutmeg and pour over the fish. Cool and cover with pastry. Brush with beaten egg. Bake at 425°F/220°C/Gas Mark 7 for 30 minutes. Cool and pack in polythene to freeze.
To serve
Reheat from frozen at 350°F/180°C/Gas Mark 4 for 50 minutes.
High Quality Storage Life   1 month

Mushroom Vol-Au-Vent

6 large frozen vol-au-vent cases
8 oz/225 g mushrooms
2 oz/50 g butter
1 oz/25 g plain flour
$\frac{3}{4}$ pint/375 ml milk
salt and pepper
2 tablespoons/30 ml single cream

Vol-au-vent cases are a useful freezer item, and save considerable time which might be spent on making your own puff pastry, or on thawing and rolling frozen slab pastry before cutting into shape and baking. Bake in a hot oven according to the directions on the packet. Meanwhile, slice or chop the mushrooms and cook them in half the butter until just tender. If large mushrooms are used, the cooking liquid and the mushrooms will be black and will make the vol-au-vent filling rather dark and unappetising. Firm button mushrooms will not become so dark during cooking, so that the finished result will be creamy and appetising. Lift out the mushrooms into a bowl. Add the remaining butter to the pan juices and then work in the flour. Cook for 1 minute and then gradually add the milk. Stir over low heat until smooth and creamy. Season to taste with salt and pepper. Just before serving, stir in the cream and the cooked mushrooms and spoon into the cooked vol-au-vent cases. Serve with vegetables. For a party, tiny vol-au-vent cases may be used with the same filling as a one-bite snack.

Asparagus Flan

8 oz/225 g short pastry
1 lb/450 g asparagus
½ pint/250 ml creamy milk
3 oz/75 g Gruyère cheese
1 oz/25 g Parmesan cheese
3 eggs
salt and pepper

Line a foil pie plate with the pastry. Bake at 400°F/ 200°C/Gas Mark 6 for 8 minutes. Cook the asparagus in boiling water, drain and cut into 2 in/5 cm lengths, keeping a few tips for decoration. Mix the milk, both the grated cheeses, eggs, salt and pepper. Put the asparagus pieces into the pastry case. Pour on the milk mixture and put the asparagus tips lightly on the surface. Bake at 350°F/180°C/Gas Mark 4 for 30 minutes. Cool and pack carefully in a box to avoid crushing. The flan may be open-frozen before being packed.

To serve
Heat at 350°F/180°C/Gas Mark 4 for 30 minutes.
High Quality Storage Life 1 month

Savoury pancakes make an unusual snack or light lunch. They are simple to prepare and are particularly useful as they take very little space in the freezer.

Savoury Pancakes

4 oz/100 g plain flour
$\frac{1}{4}$ teaspoon salt
1 egg
$\frac{1}{2}$ pint/250 ml milk
1 tablespoon/15 ml oil

Sift the flour and mix in the egg with a little milk. Work well together until creamy and gradually add the remaining milk, beating well to make a smooth batter. Fold in the oil. Fry large, thin pancakes. When cool, pack in layers, separated by Clingfilm or polythene, and pack in a polythene bag to freeze.
To serve
Separate the pancakes, put on a baking sheet covered with foil, and heat at 400°F/200°C/Gas Mark 6 for 10 minutes. Fill with a variety of savoury fillings – e.g. spinach, mushrooms, shellfish and mixed vegetables. Sprinkle with Parmesan cheese.
High Quality Storage Life   2 months

Asparagus

139

Vegetable Dishes

Ratatouille

2 medium onions
1 lb/450 g ripe tomatoes
3 small aubergines
2 small green or red peppers
4 small courgettes
2 garlic cloves
3 tablespoons/45 ml olive oil
salt and pepper

Chop the onions. Skin the tomatoes. Do not peel the aubergines, but cut them into $\frac{1}{2}$ in/1·25 cm rings. Place in a colander and sprinkle with salt. Remove the seeds and membranes from the peppers and cut the flesh into dice. Do not peel the courgettes but cut them into $\frac{1}{4}$ in/6 mm slices. Crush the garlic. Heat the oil and cook the onions and garlic until the onions are just soft and golden. Rinse the aubergines and dry the slices on kitchen paper. Add to the onion with the courgettes, tomatoes and peppers. Season with salt and pepper, cover and simmer for 45 minutes, stirring occasionally, until the oil has been absorbed. Cool, pack in a rigid container and freeze.

To serve
Thaw at room temperature for 3 hours and garnish with chopped parsley to serve cold. Ratatouille may also be reheated very gently. It is good with meat, poultry or fish, or may be served on its own as a first course.
High Quality Storage Life   2 months

Stuffed Courgettes in Tomato Sauce

6 courgettes
1 small onion
8 oz/225 g minced cooked meat
2 oz/50 g fresh breadcrumbs
salt and pepper
Sauce
14 oz/400 g canned tomatoes
1 small onion
1 garlic clove
$\frac{1}{2}$ oz/15 g butter
$\frac{1}{2}$ oz/15 g plain flour
salt and pepper

Split the courgettes in half lengthwise and place in an ovenware dish. Chop the onion very finely and mix with the meat, breadcrumbs and seasoning. Fill the courgettes with this mixture. Simmer the tomatoes in juice, finely chopped onion and crushed garlic for 10 minutes, and then put through a sieve. Melt the butter and work in the flour. Cook for 1 minute and add the sieved tomato mixture. Season well and simmer for 10 minutes. Pour over the courgettes. Cover with foil and bake for 30 minutes at 350°F/180°C/Gas Mark 4. Cool and cover with foil to freeze (the dish may be cooked in a foil container and then covered with a card lid if preferred).
To serve
Cover with foil and heat at 350°F/180°C/Gas Mark 4 for 30 minutes. Remove foil and continue heating for 15 minutes.
High Quality Storage Life   2 months

Stuffed courgettes make a tasty light lunch for one and are very simple to prepare.

Ratatouille is a mixture of summer vegetables and can be eaten either hot or cold. It is a good way of preserving these vegetables.

Bean casserole is a delicious winter dish which freezes very well.

Bean Casserole

12 oz/375 g butter beans
3 pints/1½ litres water
1 glass red wine
12 oz/375 g bacon
2 garlic cloves
salt and pepper
12 oz/375 g potatoes
10 oz/300 g runner beans
4 tomatoes
parsley

Soak the butter beans overnight in the water. The next day, add the wine and the bacon, bring to the boil, and simmer for 1 hour. Crush the garlic clove with salt and add to the pot. Season with salt and pepper. Peel the potatoes and slice, add to the pot and simmer for a further 10 minutes. Then add the runner beans. Simmer for a further 15 minutes. Leave to cool and freeze.

To serve

Reheat thoroughly. 5 minutes before serving add the sliced tomatoes and chopped parsley.

High Quality Storage Life   2 months

Mixed vegetable casserole is an ideal way to use home-grown vegetables throughout the year.

OVERLEAF: *Stuffed aubergine are an unusual freezer item, and are delicious with a slice of cheese melted on top.*

Mixed Vegetable Casserole

2 lb/1 kg assorted vegetables e.g. a mixture of
    carrots, parsnips, potatoes, onions, celery,
    peppers and tomatoes
3 rashers bacon
2 oz/50 g butter
2 oz/50 g flour
1 tablespoon made mustard
½ pint/250 ml milk
3 oz/75 g grated cheese

Peel all the vegetables, dice and cook in boiling salted water for 10 minutes. Drain and reserve ½ pint/250 ml of the vegetable stock. Derind the bacon rashers, cut into strips and dry fry. Melt butter in a pan, remove from the heat and stir in the flour and mustard. Add the milk and vegetable stock and bring to the boil, stirring continuously. Simmer for 10 minutes until thick. Pour half the sauce on the bottom of a foil freezer dish, add the cooked vegetables and bacon pieces. Season well with salt and pepper and cover with the rest of the sauce. Sprinkle the grated cheese on top. Bake for 20 minutes at 350°F/180°C/Gas Mark 4. Cool, cover with a lid and freeze.
To serve
Uncover, and heat at 350°F/180°C/Gas Mark 4 for 35 minutes.
High Quality Storage Life   1 month

Stuffed Aubergines

2 aubergines
salt
1½ oz/40 g cooked rice
2 oz/50 g chopped ham
1 teaspoon chopped onion
1 teaspoon chopped parsley
1 oz/25 g butter
1 oz/25 g chopped mushrooms
½ teaspoon grated lemon rind
1 egg
salt and pepper
4 slices Cheddar cheese

Wipe the aubergines and cut them in half lengthwise. Scoop out the seeds and sprinkle the insides well with salt. Let them lie, cut side downwards for an hour. Mix together the rice, ham, onion, parsley, softened butter, mushrooms, lemon rind, egg, salt and pepper. Drain the aubergines and wipe them. Fill them with the stuffing, piling it high, and place them in a greased foil freezer container. Cover with a piece of greased paper (butter paper will do). Bake at 350°F/180°C/Gas Mark 4 for 45 minutes. Cool, cover and freeze.
To serve
Remove cover, place a slice of cheese on each stuffed aubergine, and heat at 350°F/180°C/Gas Mark 4 for 20 minutes. This is good served with a hot tomato sauce.
High Quality Storage Life   1 month

Stuffed onion

Stuffed Onions

4 large onions
8 oz/225 g cooked minced beef or lamb
2 oz/50 g fresh breadcrumbs
¼ pint/125 ml brown gravy
1 teaspoon/5 ml tomato purée

Peel the onions and boil until just tender. Remove
centres and chop finely. Mix with meat, breadcrumbs and gravy, tomato purée, salt and pepper.
Fill onions with this mixture and put into a baking
tin with a little dripping. Sprinkle with a few breadcrumbs and bake at 400°F/200°C/Gas Mark 6 for 45
minutes, basting well. Cool. Pack in foil tray,
covering with foil.
To serve
Heat at 350°F/180°C/Gas Mark 4 for 45 minutes and
serve with gravy.
High Quality Storage Life   1 month

Baked Leeks

16 large or 24 small leeks
water or chicken stock
5 tablespoons butter
2 tablespoons/30 ml double cream
salt and black pepper

Preheat oven at 350°F/180°C/Gas Mark 4. Prepare
the leeks and put in a large pan. Add water or
chicken stock barely to cover, and simmer with lid
on for 5 minutes. Drain leeks and transfer to a foil
freezer dish. Add butter and cream and bake, turning occasionally, for 10 minutes. Season with salt
and pepper to taste. Cool, cover and freeze.
To serve
Uncover sprinkle with grated cheese, cover with a
rasher of bacon and heat at 350°F/180°C/Gas Mark
4 for 35 minutes.
High Quality Storage Life   1 month

Baked leeks

Stuffed artichoke

Stuffed Artichokes

4 globe artichokes
½ pint/250 ml stock
4 oz/100 g cooked ham
2 oz/50 g frozen peas
1 small onion
1 garlic clove

Clean artichokes and cook them in boiling water until tender (frozen ones can be used). Mince the ham and chop the onion. Mix together the ham, peas, onion and crushed garlic and stuff the artichokes. Put the stock into a foil freezer container, and pack the artichokes in close together. Cover and cook at 350°F/180°C/Gas Mark 4 for 20 minutes. Cool, cover and freeze.

To serve
Remove cover and heat at 350°F/180°C/Gas Mark 4 for 20 minutes. Add butter, salt and pepper and continue heating for 15 minutes: Lift on to a dish, and garnish with a prawn. Serve the liquid separately.
High Quality Storage Life 2 months

Beans in Tomato Sauce

2 tablespoons/30 ml olive oil
1 large onion
1 small green pepper
8 oz/225 g tomatoes
1 teaspoon salt
$\frac{1}{4}$ teaspoon black pepper
bay leaf
pinch of marjoram
1$\frac{1}{2}$ lb/675 g French beans
1 garlic clove, crushed

Heat the oil in a pan. Chop the onion and pepper, and toss these in the oil for 10 minutes. Peel the tomatoes and chop into small pieces. Add to the onions, together with the salt, pepper and herbs. Bring to the boil and then simmer for 20 minutes. Cut the beans into pieces and add them to the tomatoes. Simmer over a low heat for 20 minutes, add the garlic and continue cooking for 10 minutes. Cool and pack into rigid container to freeze.
To serve
Turn into a pan, cover and cook slowly till thawed.
High Quality Storage Life   2 months

Sweet and Sour Red Cabbage

$\frac{1}{2}$ oz/15 g butter
1 medium onion
1 tablespoon brown sugar
1 tablespoon/15 ml cider vinegar
2 lb/1 kg red cabbage
salt and pepper
$\frac{1}{4}$ pint/125 ml cider
2 small tart apples

Melt the butter and fry the sliced onion until soft. Add the sugar, vinegar and the cabbage which has been finely shredded. Add salt and pepper and the cider and cover tightly. Simmer for 1 hour. Peel and core the apples and cut them into slices. Stir into the cabbage and continue cooking for 1 hour. Pack into rigid container and freeze.
To serve
Heat gently in a double saucepan, or in a moderate oven, and serve with pork, bacon or goose.
High Quality Storage Life   2 months

Potato Croquettes

2 lb/1 kg potatoes
$\frac{3}{4}$ teaspoon salt
pinch of white pepper
1 oz/25 g butter
2 eggs or 2 egg yolks
3 fl. oz/75 ml milk
1 tablespoon/15 ml salad oil
$1\frac{1}{2}$ oz/40 g plain flour
2 oz/50 g dry breadcrumbs

Peel the potatoes and cut them in small pieces. Cook them in boiling salted water until tender, and drain well. Shake over a low heat until they are dry and then mash them smoothly. Beat in the salt and pepper, butter, 1 egg and the egg yolks. Form into sausage shapes (this amount will make about 10 croquettes). Beat the remaining egg with the milk and oil. Dip the croquettes into the flour, then into the egg mixture and the breadcrumbs. Put on to a tray or baking sheet and open-freeze. Pack in a rigid container with foil or film between the layers.
To serve
Fry frozen croquettes in deep fat until golden. Drain well before serving.
High Quality Storage Life   2 months

It is simple to make croquettes for freezing with leftover boiled potatoes.

OVERLEAF: *A wide selection of fresh vegetables can be served all year with the use of a freezer.*

Stuffed peppers with a meat filling are particularly delicious served with a tomato sauce.

Spinach flan is unusual and may be served on its own or with thin slices of cooked ham or hard boiled eggs.

Stuffed Peppers

4 large green or red peppers
1 oz/25 g butter
8 oz/225 g raw minced beef
1 small onion
3 oz/75 g cooked long-grain rice
1 teaspoon marjoram
2 teaspoons chopped parsley
2 teaspoons/10 ml concentrated tomato purée
2 tablespoons/30 ml stock or water
salt and pepper

Slice the top off each pepper and remove seeds and membranes. Put the peppers into a pan and cover with boiling water. Boil for 5 minutes and drain well. Melt the butter and brown the meat with the finely chopped onion. Remove from the heat and stir in the rice, the chopped tops of the peppers, herbs, tomato purée and stock or water. Season well with salt and pepper. Fill the peppers with the mixture and place them in a greased foil container. Bake at 350°F/180°C/Gas Mark 4 for 30 minutes. Cool, cover with a lid and freeze.

Remove lid and heat peppers at 350°F/180°C/Gas Mark 4 for 45 minutes. Serve with additional tomato sauce if liked.

High Quality Storage Life 2 months

Spinach Flan

1 lb/450 g shortcrust pastry
1½ lb/750 g spinach
2 oz/50 g butter
2 eggs
8 oz/225 g full fat soft cream cheese
2 oz/50 g Parmesan cheese
salt and pepper
pinch of ground nutmeg

Line a 10 in/25 cm flan ring with the pastry. Prick with a fork, line with foil and fill with baking beans. Bake at 425°F/220°C/Gas Mark 7 for 10 minutes. Remove foil and beans and continue baking for 5 minutes. Cool and place on a cake board. Wash the spinach very well and then put into a pan with the butter. Cover and cook for about 8 minutes until soft. Drain well and press out excess moisture. Put into a bowl and add the eggs and cream cheese beaten together. Stir in the grated Parmesan cheese, salt, pepper and nutmeg. Put into the pastry case. Open-freeze until firm and then wrap in foil for storage.

To serve
Unwrap and return flan to flan ring. Bake from frozen at 450°F/230°C/Gas Mark 8 for 15 minutes, and then at 375°F/190°C/Gas Mark 5 for 25 minutes. Leave to stand for 5 minutes before removing flan ring, and serve hot or cold.

High Quality Storage Life 1 month

Sauces and Stuffings

Tomato Sauce

1 lb/450 g ripe tomatoes
1 oz/25 g butter
1 small onion
1 small carrot
1 oz/25 g ham
1 pint/500 ml stock
Sprig of parsley
Sprig of thyme
1 bay leaf
1 oz/25 g cornflour

Cut the tomatoes in slices. Melt the butter and fry sliced onion and carrot until soft and golden. Add the tomatoes, chopped ham, stock and herbs and simmer for 30 minutes. Put through a sieve, and return to a clean saucepan. Mix the cornflour with a little water and stir into the sauce. Simmer for 5 minutes, stirring well. Cool and pack in a rigid container to freeze.
To serve
Reheat in a double saucepan, or in a bowl over hot water, stirring gently.
High Quality Storage Life   12 months

Basic Poultry Stuffing

2 oz/50 g shredded suet
4 oz/100 g fresh breadcrumbs
2 teaspoons chopped parsley
1 teaspoon chopped thyme
1 teaspoon grated lemon peel
salt and pepper
1 egg

Mix all the ingredients, beginning with the beaten egg. Pack into a polythene bag for freezer storage.

To serve
Thaw in refrigerator for 2 hours and then stuff the bird. This stuffing may also be used for whole fish such as haddock, cod or mackerel.
High Quality Storage Life   1 month

Gooseberry Sauce

1 lb/450 g gooseberries
2 tablespoons/30 ml water
1 oz/25 g butter
2 oz/50 g sugar

Wash the gooseberries but do not top and tail them. Put them into a pan with the water and butter, cover and cook for 15 minutes on low heat. When the berries are soft, put through a sieve, extracting as much liquid as possible. Reheat the purée with the sugar, stirring until it has dissolved. Cool and pack in small containers to freeze.
To serve
Reheat gently and use with fish, or with ices or steamed puddings.
High Quality Storage Life   3 months

Apple Sauce

apples
water or dry cider
sugar
lemon juice

Slice the apples without peeling them. Put them into a casserole with just enough water or dry cider to cover them. Cover and cook at 325°F/170°C/Gas Mark 3 for 45 minutes until the apples are soft. Put through a sieve and sweeten to taste, adding a good squeeze of lemon juice. Do not oversweeten, as apple sauce is usually needed as an accompaniment for duck or pork. Cool and pack into small rigid containers, and freeze.

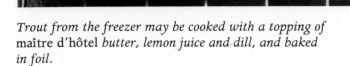

Trout from the freezer may be cooked with a topping of maître d'hôtel butter, lemon juice and dill, and baked in foil.

To serve
Thaw for 3 hours at room temperature.
High Quality Storage Life   12 months

Maître d'Hôtel Butter

2 oz/50 g butter
2 teaspoons/10 ml lemon juice
2 teaspoons chopped parsley
salt and pepper

Cream the butter and work in the other ingredients. Form the butter into a cylinder and wrap in grease-proof paper or polythene, then freeze.
To serve
Unwrap the butter and cut the cylinder in slices to form round pats. Serve on grilled meat or fish, or on vegetables.
High Quality Storage Life   2 months

Maître d'hôtel butter is easily made and makes a professional garnish for grilled meat and fish.

155

Parsley sauce

Piquant Parsley Sauce

2 × 5 oz/125 g cartons soured cream
grated rind and juice of ½ small lemon
2 teaspoons/10 ml tomato purée
3 tablespoons chopped parsley
salt and pepper

Combine all ingredients and season to taste. Spoon into rigid container, cover, label and freeze.
To serve
Thaw for 3 hours at room temperature or 8 hours in refrigerator, whisk well and adjust seasoning.
High Quality Storage Life　2 months

Sausage Stuffing

1 lb/450 g sausage meat
2 oz/50 g streaky bacon
liver from turkey or chicken
1 onion
1 egg
2 oz/50 g fresh white breadcrumbs
salt and pepper
2 teaspoons fresh mixed herbs stock

Put sausage meat in a bowl. Mince bacon, liver and onion. Mix with sausage meat, egg, breadcrumbs, seasoning and herbs, and moisten with a little stock if necessary. Do not stuff bird in advance with sausage stuffing. Pack in cartons or polythene bags.
To serve
Thaw in refrigerator for 12 hours before using to stuff bird.
High Quality Storage Life　2 weeks

Cranberry Sauce

1 lb/450 g cranberries
¾ pint/375 ml water
¾ lb/350 g sugar

Rinse the cranberries. Dissolve sugar in water over gentle heat, add cranberries and cook gently for 15 minutes until cranberries pop. Cool. Pack in small waxed containers.
To serve
Thaw at room temperature for 3 hours.
High Quality Storage Life　1 year

156

Hot Tartare Sauce

1 oz/25 g butter
1 oz/25 g flour
½ pint/250 ml milk
1 teaspoon capers
1 teaspoon chopped gherkins
1 teaspoon chopped parsley
salt and pepper

Melt butter in pan, stir in flour and cook gently for 2 minutes. Add milk and slowly bring to boil, stirring continuously until sauce thickens. Add remaining ingredients and season to taste. Pour into rigid container, seal, label and freeze.
To serve
Heat gently in double saucepan and stir until sauce melts and just comes to boiling point.
High Quality Storage Life   2 months

Orange Stuffing

6 oz/150 g breadcrumbs
2 large oranges
2 oz/50 g melted butter
1 teaspoon celery salt
1 egg
1 teaspoon chopped parsley
1 teaspoon chopped sage

Put the breadcrumbs into a mixing bowl. Grate the peel from the oranges and squeeze the juice from one of them. Strip all the pith from the other orange and cut the sections into small pieces. Mix the orange sections, rind and juice, breadcrumbs, butter, celery salt, egg, parsley and sage thoroughly. Pack in cartons or polythene bags.
To serve
Thaw in refrigerator for 12 hours before stuffing duck.
High Quality Storage Life   1 month

Chestnut Stuffing

1 lb/450 g chestnuts
2 oz/50 g fresh white breadcrumbs
1 oz/25 g melted butter
2 teaspoons fresh mixed herbs
2 eggs
salt, pepper and dry mustard

Chestnuts

Peel chestnuts, then simmer in a little milk until tender. Sieve and mix with breadcrumbs, butter, herbs and eggs. Add salt and pepper and a pinch of dry mustard. Pack in cartons or polythene bags.
To serve
Thaw in refrigerator for 12 hours before stuffing bird.
High Quality Storage Life   1 month

Cherry Stuffing

5 oz/125 g breadcrumbs
5 oz/125 g sausage meat
3 oz/75 g grated apple
2½ oz/60 g maraschino cherries
1 egg
salt and pepper

Mix the breadcrumbs, sausage meat and apple. Cut the cherries in half and add to the breadcrumbs, together with the egg, salt and pepper. Pack in cartons or polythene bags.
To serve
Thaw in refrigerator for 12 hours before stuffing duck.
High Quality Storage Life   2 weeks

Puddings

Fruit Flan Pastry

6 oz/150 g plain flour
pinch of salt
1 tablespoon icing sugar
3 oz/75 g butter
2 egg yolks
1 tablespoon/15 ml iced water

Sift the flour, salt and sugar on to a board. Make a well in the centre and put in the butter cut into small pieces. Add the egg yolks and work together with a palette knife until the mixture is like breadcrumbs. Sprinkle in the water and knead the dough on a lightly floured board until smooth. Chill in the refrigerator for 30 minutes and then roll out carefully to fit a 9 in/22·5 cm flan tin. Prick with a fork, line with foil and fill with baking beans. Bake at 425°F/220°C/Gas Mark 7 for 15 minutes. Remove the foil and beans and continue baking for about 10 minutes until the pastry is crisp and golden. Cool and wrap in foil to freeze.
To serve
Unwrap and thaw on a serving plate at room temperature for 1 hour. Arrange circles of fruit in the flan case and brush thickly with hot sieved apricot jam or redcurrant jelly.
High Quality Storage Life   4 months

Berkshire Pigs

8 oz/225 g shortcrust pastry
1 large eating apple
2 oz/50 g currants
1 oz/25 g soft brown sugar
1 teaspoon ground mixed spice
2 teaspoons chopped mixed peel
1 oz/25 g butter

Roll out the pastry into a rectangle and cut into three oblong pieces. Peel and chop the apple. Mix the

Fruit flan pastry – a sweet pastry case from the freezer may be filled with a variety of fruits and glazed with apricot jam.

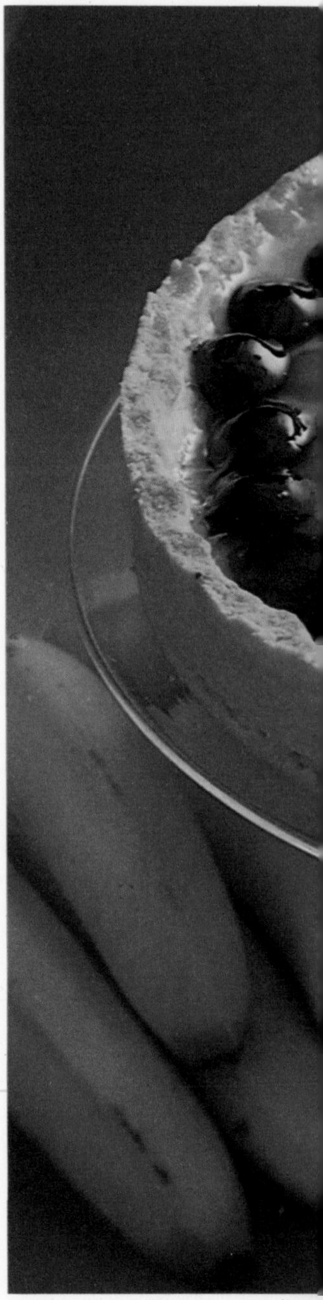

apple, currants, sugar, spice and peel and divide the mixture between the three pieces of pastry. Put a small piece of butter on each. Fold the pastry so that the join is on the top and pinch together to make an edge on the 'backbone'. Pull out one end of the roll to form a tail, and the other end to form a head. Put three currants for eyes and nose. Form small pieces of pastry for ears. Bake at 400°F/200°C/Gas Mark 6 for 25 minutes. Pack in polythene to freeze.

To serve

Thaw at room temperature for 4 hours to eat cold, or reheat from frozen at 350°F/180°C/Gas Mark 4 for 35 minutes.

High Quality Storage Life   2 months

Raspberry tart is made with cinammon-flavoured pastry and has a decorative lattice topping.

Raspberry Tart

6 oz/150 g plain flour
pinch of ground cinnamon
pinch of salt
4 oz/100 g butter
4 oz/100 g caster sugar
1 egg yolk
4 oz/100 g almonds or walnuts
grated peel of 1 lemon
8 oz/225 g raspberry jam (or sweetened
   raspberry pulp)
beaten egg to glaze

Sieve the flour and cinnamon on to a board with a pinch of salt. Make a well in the centre and put in the butter cut in small pieces, with the sugar, egg and egg yolk. Do not blanch the nuts but chop them very finely in a blender. Put with the other ingredients and the lemon rind and work them together using a palette knife to form a soft dough. Chill in the refrigerator for 1 hour. Roll out very carefully $\frac{1}{2}$ in/1·25 cm thick and line a flan ring, trimming the edges. Fill the pastry case with jam or raspberry pulp. Roll out the pastry trimmings and cut strips. Arrange them to form a lattice. Brush with beaten egg and bake at 375°F/190°C/Gas Mark 5 for 30 minutes. Cool and wrap in foil or polythene for freezer storage.

To serve
Thaw at room temperature for 3 hours and dust with icing sugar just before serving.
High Quality Storage Life   4 months

Chocolate Ice Cream

½ pint/250 ml milk
2 egg yolks
4 oz/100 g sugar
4 oz/100 g plain chocolate
1 teaspoon instant coffee powder
¼ pint/125 ml double cream

Bring the milk almost to boiling point. Beat the egg yolks and sugar until creamy, and pour on the milk, beating well. Return the mixture to the saucepan and stir over very low heat until the mixture forms a creamy custard. Put the chocolate and coffee powder into a bowl over hot water and heat until melted. Add this chocolate mixture to the custard and cool, stirring occasionally. Whip the cream to soft peaks and fold into the chocolate mixture. Put into a freezing tray and freeze with the refrigerator at lowest setting for 3 hours, beating once half-way through freezing. For freezer storage, make the ice cream completely, and then pack into a rigid container.

Chocolate ice-cream is always a great favourite and makes a really special dish garnished with whipped cream and cocktail cherries.

To serve
Remove to refrigerator for 30 minutes before serving so that the flavour mellows. Scoop into serving dishes and garnish with whipped cream.
High Quality Storage Life   1 month

Blackcurrant Pie

8 oz/225 g shortcrust pastry
1 lb/450 g blackcurrants
4 oz/100 g soft brown sugar
2 teaspoons plain flour
a little cold milk
a little caster sugar

Roll out the pastry and use half to line a foil pie plate. Mix the currants with the sugar and flour and put on the pastry base. Cover with the remaining pastry and seal the edges firmly. Brush with a little milk and sprinkle with sugar. Bake at 425°F/220°C/Gas Mark 7 for 15 minutes, then reduce to 350°F/180°C/Gas Mark 4 for 20 minutes. Cool completely, wrap in foil or polythene and freeze.
To serve
Thaw at room temperature for 3 hours to serve cold or reheat from frozen at 350°F/180°C/Gas Mark 4 for 40 minutes.
High Quality Storage Life   4 months

Cherry Crumble

1½ lb/750 g stoned cherries
5 tablespoons/75 ml water
1 oz/25 g caster sugar
4 oz/100 g self-raising flour
2 oz/50 g butter
2 oz/50 g soft brown sugar
pinch of ground mixed spice

Gooseberries or blackcurrants are also good for this crumble, but may need a little more sugar to sweeten them. Put the cherries, water and sugar into a freezer-proof pie dish. Mix the butter into the flour and rub until the mixture is like fine breadcrumbs. Stir in the sugar and spice and mix thoroughly. Sprinkle on top of the cherries. Bake at 375°F/190°C/Gas Mark 5 for 45 minutes until the top is golden. Cool and cover with foil or polythene to freeze. The crumble may be frozen uncooked, but as it is good to eat cold, it is more useful to store it ready-cooked.
To serve
Thaw at room temperature for 4 hours to eat cold with cream, or reheat at 350°F/180°C/Gas Mark 4 for 45 minutes to serve hot with custard.
High Quality Storage Life   4 months

Bread Pudding

8 oz/225 g stale white bread
1½ oz/40 g shredded suet
1 oz/25 g chopped mixed peel
2 oz/50 g sultanas
2 oz/50 g currants
½ teaspoon ground allspice
pinch of ground nutmeg
1½ oz/40 g sugar
1 egg
1 fl. oz/25 ml milk

Break the bread into small pieces and soak in cold water until soft. Drain and squeeze out surplus liquid. Mix the suet, peel, dried fruit, spices and sugar with the bread and beat in the egg and milk. Put into a greased roasting tin or foil dish and bake at 325°F/170°C/Gas Mark 3 for 2 hours. If made in a foil dish, put on a lid for freezing; if made in a roasting tin, turn out and wrap in polythene to freeze.

To serve

Thaw at room temperature for 3 hours to serve in the traditional manner as a cake, cut in squares. For a pudding, reheat in a low oven when thawed and serve with custard.

High Quality Storage Life   2 months

Pancakes are a useful standby to have in the freezer. Here they are filled with jam and sprinkled with finely chopped nuts.

Pancakes

4 oz/100 g plain flour
$\frac{1}{4}$ teaspoon salt
1 egg
1 egg yolk
$\frac{1}{2}$ pint/250 ml milk
1 tablespoon oil or melted butter

Sift the flour and salt and mix in the egg and egg yolk with a little milk. Work together until creamy and gradually add remaining milk, beating to a smooth batter. Fold in the oil or melted butter. Fry large thin pancakes. When cool/ pack in layers separated by Clingfilm and put into a polythene bag to freeze.

To serve
Separate the pancakes, put on a baking sheet and cover with foil. Heat at 400°F/200°C/Gas Mark 6 for 10 minutes, and fill with jam, or serve with sugar and lemon juice. The pancakes may also be thawed at room temperature and filled with a savoury filling, then covered with a cheese, mushroom or tomato sauce for reheating.
High Quality Storage Life   2 months

Lemon Cheesecake

Base
3 oz/75 g margarine
1 oz/25 g soft brown sugar
4 oz/100 g digestive biscuits
Cheesecake
8 oz/225 g full fat soft cream cheese
3 oz/75 g caster sugar
2 eggs
⅓ pint/150 ml lemon yogurt
juice and peel of ½ lemon
½ oz/15 g gelatine
4 tablespoons/60 ml water
¼ pint/125 ml double cream

If lemon yogurt is not available, use natural yogurt and then use the juice and rind of 1 lemon. Make the base by melting the margarine and sugar together and stirring in the finely crushed biscuits. Press into the base of a greased 8 in/20 cm cake tin with removable base, and leave in a cold place for a few minutes until firm. Cream the cheese and sugar until smooth and gradually work in the egg yolks, yogurt, lemon rind and juice. Dissolve the gelatine in water and heat gently until syrupy. Cool slightly and add to the cheese mixture. Whip the cream lightly and fold into the mixture. Whisk the egg whites to soft peaks and fold into the mixture. Pour on top of the base and chill until firm. Remove from the tin, leaving the cheesecake on the metal base. Open-freeze and when firm, turn upside down on to a piece of foil. Ease away the metal base of the cake tin. Wrap the foil round the cheesecake and store.
To serve
Thaw in refrigerator without wrappings for 6 hours. Decorate if liked with whipped cream, fresh or canned fruit, or grated chocolate.
High Quality Storage Life   2 months

Baked Apple Dumplings

8 oz/225 g shortcrust pastry
4 small cooking apples
1 oz/25 g seedless raisins
1 oz/25 g brown sugar
1 oz/25 g softened butter
¼ teaspoon ground cinnamon

Roll out the pastry and cut into four squares. Peel and core the apples and put one in the centre of each piece of pastry. Fill centres of apples with a mixture of raisins, sugar, butter and cinnamon. Enclose the apples completely in pastry, sealing edges well. Brush over with a little beaten egg or milk and bake at 425°F/220°C/Gas Mark 7 for 25 minutes. Cool and

Cheesecake flavoured with lemon and made from full-fat soft cheese is really delicious when just thawed.

pack in a foil tray. Cover with foil and freeze.
To serve
Thaw at room temperature for 3 hours to serve cold, or reheat if liked. Sprinkle with caster sugar or serve with hot apricot jam or custard.
High Quality Storage Life   4 months

Cheesecake with Raspberries

2 oz/50 g margarine
8 oz/225 g digestive biscuits
12 oz/350 g full fat soft cream cheese
3 oz/75 g caster sugar
2 eggs
1 lemon
1 packet gelatine
2 tablespoons/30 ml water
½ pint/250 ml double cream
1 lb/450 g raspberries (for serving)

Melt the margarine and stir in the crushed biscuit crumbs. Press into a greased 9 in/22·5 cm cake tin with a removable bottom. Bake at 350°F/180°C/Gas

164

Cheesecake with raspberries is made from a frozen cheesecake, topped with fresh or frozen fruit as it thaws.

Mark 4 for 10 minutes and cool. Cream the cheese with the sugar and egg yolks until light and fluffy. Add the grated lemon peel. Dissolve the gelatine in the water and heat gently until syrupy. Stir in the juice of the lemon and beat into the cream cheese mixture. Whisk the egg whites until stiff and whip the cream to soft peaks. Fold the cream into the cheese mixture and finally fold in the egg whites. Chill and then open freeze until solid. Remove from tin and wrap in foil for storage.

To serve
Unwrap and thaw at room temperature for 3 hours. Top with fresh or frozen raspberries and continue thawing for 1 hour.
High Quality Storage Life 2 months

Crunchy Apricot Crumble

8 oz/225 g cooked or canned apricots
2 oz/50 g caster sugar
2 oz/50 g plain flour
½ teaspoon baking powder
2 oz/50 g porridge oats
3 oz/75 g Demerara sugar
2 oz/50 g soft margarine

Arrange apricots in an ovenware container and sprinkle with sugar. Mix together remaining ingredients and sprinkle over the fruit. Cover and freeze.

To serve
Remove lid and bake at 400°F/200°C/Gas Mark 6 for 45 minutes and serve with cream or ice cream.
High Quality Storage Life 4 months

Waffles

4 oz/100 g self-raising flour
pinch of salt
1 tablespoon/15 g caster sugar
1 egg, separated
2 tablespoons butter, melted
$\frac{1}{4}$ pint/125 ml milk

Mix the ingredients together in a bowl. Add the egg yolk, melted butter and milk, and beat well to a smooth batter. Whisk the egg white stiffly and fold into the batter.

Pour enough batter into a waffle iron to run over the surface. Do not overfill or the mixture will spill, and the waffle will not be able to rise properly. Close the iron over the mixture and leave to cook for 2–3 minutes, turning once. Waffles for freezing should not be over-brown. Leave to cool, and pack in foil or polythene.

To serve
Heat unthawed under a grill or in a hot oven. Serve with a choice of maple syrup (the traditional accompaniment), golden syrup, or melted butter; or sandwich with layers of jam, whipped cream and redcurrant jelly, and dredged with icing sugar.
High Quality Storage Life 2 months

Ice Cream Sundaes

Ice cream sundaes can be made from any combination of homemade or shop bought ice cream and either fresh or frozen fruits and fruit syrups.

Waffles are delicious sandwiched with jam and cream.

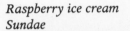

Raspberry ice cream Sundae

Nut ice-cream may be shaped in a bowl for cutting into slices and then garnished with crushed nut toffee.

Nut Ice Cream

6 oz/150 g mixed nuts
6 oz/150 g caster sugar
pinch of salt
1 pint/500 ml double cream
2 eggs
1 teaspoon/5 ml vanilla essence

Use a mixture of nuts such as walnuts, almonds and and hazelnuts. Blanch them in hot water and rub off the skins. Chop the nuts fairly finely. Mix the sugar, salt and nuts and stir in the cream gradually. Put into the top of a double saucepan, or into a bowl over hot water and cook for 10 minutes. Take off the heat and stir in the beaten eggs and essence gradually. Cool and pour into a freezer tray. Freeze for 1 hour, then beat well and return to freezer tray. Freeze for about 2 hours until firm. Scoop into a bowl or foil pudding basin and press down well. Cover with foil or a lid to store in the freezer. If liked, coffee essence may be used instead of vanilla.
To serve
Remove to refrigerator for 30 minutes before serving. Unmould and serve with whipped cream.
High Quality Storage Life   1 month

Tangerine ice is served in the fruit skins and garnished with marzipan leaves to make a delicious light finish to a meal.

Tangerine Ice

4 large tangerines
1 teaspoon gelatine
¼ pint/125 ml water
3 oz/75 g sugar
1 teaspoon grated lemon peel
1 tablespoon/15 ml lemon juice
1 egg white

Remove the tops of the tangerines carefully so that they will form lids. Scoop out the flesh, saving all the juice. Wash the skins carefully and dry them. Soak the gelatine in a little of the water and boil the rest with the sugar for 5 minutes to a syrup. Stir the gelatine into the syrup and leave to cool. Add the grated lemon peel and juice, and all the juice of the tangerines. Beat the egg white to stiff peaks and fold fold into the gelatine mixture. Put into a freezing tray and freeze with the refrigerator at lowest setting for 3 hours, beating once half-way through freezing when the ice is mushy. Scoop the ice into the tangerine cases and put the lids on lightly. Put into the freezer for 1 hour before serving, and garnish with mint leaves, or small green marzipan leaves. For longer storage, wrap tangerines in foil.
High Quality Storage Life   1 month

Sliced Apple Tart

6 oz/150 g plain flour
4 oz/100 g butter
3 tablespoons/45 ml milk
2 oz/50 g brown sugar
2 oz/50 g mixed dried fruit
½ teaspoon mixed spice
1 oz/25 g chopped mixed peel
1½ lb/675 g apples
2 tablespoons/25 g fresh white breadcrumbs

Rub the butter into the flour and mix to a dough with the milk. Roll out to a rectangle about 10 × 6 in (25 × 15 cm) and put on a greased baking sheet. Peel and slice the apples fairly thickly and mix with sugar, dried fruit, spice, peel and crumbs. Put down the centre of the pastry, leaving about 2 in/5 cm at each side. Fold these sides over the fruit mixture, leaving the centre visible. Bake at 350°F/180°C/Gas Mark 4 for 40 minutes. Cool and pack in foil or polythene to freeze.

To serve

Thaw at room temperature for 3 hours to serve cold, or reheat if liked to serve with cream, ice cream or custard.

High Quality Storage Life   4 months

Breads, Cakes and Pastries

Welsh Teacakes

8 oz/225 g self-raising flour
5 oz/125 g butter
1 egg
4 oz/100 g sugar
3 oz/75 g currants
2 oz/50 g sultanas
$\frac{1}{4}$ teaspoon ground ginger
$\frac{1}{2}$ teaspoon grated lemon peel
milk to mix

Rub the fat into the flour until the mixture is like fine breadcrumbs, and stir in the egg, sugar, currants, sultanas, ginger and peel. Add a little milk to make a stiff dough. Roll out $\frac{1}{4}$ in/6 mm thick. Cut into rounds and cook in a heavy frying pan which has been lightly greased. Turn once during cooking. Cool on a wire rack and pack in a polythene bag to freeze.
To serve
Thaw at room temperature for 2 hours, or reheat if liked. Sprinkle with caster sugar before serving.
High Quality Storage Life   4 months

Family Fruit Cake

8 oz/225 g self-raising flour
$\frac{1}{4}$ teaspoon salt
4 oz/100 g butter
4 oz/100 g soft brown sugar
4 oz/100 g sultanas and raisins
2 oz/50 g chopped mixed peel
grated rind of $\frac{1}{2}$ lemon
1 egg
5 tablespoons/75 ml milk

Sift flour and salt and then rub in butter until the mixture looks like fine breadcrumbs. Stir in sugar, dried fruit, peel and grated rind, and mix lightly with beaten egg and milk. Put into a greased and lined 6 in/15 cm cake tin. Bake at 350°F/180°C/Gas Mark 4 for 1$\frac{1}{2}$ hours. Cool on a wire rack. Wrap in polythene to freeze.
To serve
Thaw at room temperature for 3 hours.
High Quality Storage Life   4 months

Hermits

4 oz/100 g butter
6 oz/150 g soft brown sugar
2 eggs
8 oz/225 g plain flour
$\frac{1}{2}$ teaspoon salt
1 teaspoon baking powder
1 teaspoon ground cinnamon
$\frac{1}{4}$ teaspoon ground cloves
$\frac{1}{4}$ teaspoon ground nutmeg
10 oz/250 g seedless raisins
3 oz/75 g chopped nuts

Cream the butter and sugar, add eggs and beat until light and fluffy. Add all the other ingredients and mix well. Drop in teaspoonfuls on greased baking sheets. Bake at 350°F/180°C/Gas Mark 4 for 10 minutes. Cool on a wire rack and pack in polythene bags to freeze.
To serve
Thaw at room temperature for 2 hours.
High Quality Storage Life   4 months

Coffee Fruit Buns

12 oz/350 g self-raising flour
pinch of salt
3 oz/75 g butter
5 oz/125 g soft brown sugar
1$\frac{1}{2}$ oz/40 g sultanas
2 teaspoons/10 g coffee powder
1 egg
$\frac{1}{4}$ pint/125 ml milk

Sieve the flour and salt together and rub in the butter. Sir in the sugar and sultanas. Mix the coffee, egg and milk together and then mix with the dry ingredients. Mix thoroughly and divide into 18 pieces. Roll each into a ball and flatten slightly on greased baking sheets. Bake at 375°F/190°C/Gas Mark 5 for 15 minutes. Cool on a rack and pack in a polythene bag to freeze.

To serve
Thaw at room temperature for 1 hour. If liked, ice with a little coffee or lemon water icing.
High Quality Storage Life   4 months

Banana Bread

2 oz/50 g soft margarine
3 bananas
4 oz/100 g caster sugar
1 egg
6 tablespoons/90 ml milk
grated rind of 1 orange
2 oz/50 g walnuts
10 oz/300 g plain flour
1 teaspoon baking powder
¼ teaspoon bicarbonate of soda
½ teaspoon salt

Put the margarine into a bowl and add the bananas cut into small pieces. Mash thoroughly so that the bananas are completely broken up. Add all the remaining ingredients, chopping the walnuts finely. Beat well and put into a 2 lb/1 kg loaf tin, lined on the bottom with greaseproof paper. Bake at 350°F/180°C/Gas Mark 4 for 1½ hours. Cool on a wire rack. Pack in foil or polythene to freeze.

To serve
Thaw at room temperature for 3 hours.
High Quality Storage Life   4 months

Ginger Fruit Cake

8 oz/225 g self-raising flour
½ teaspoon salt
2 teaspoons ground ginger
1 teaspoon ground cinnamon
4 oz/100 g butter
4 oz/100 g caster sugar
1 egg
1 tablespoon/15 ml black treacle
¼ teaspoon bicarbonate of soda
scant ½ pint/250 ml milk
6 oz/150 g sultanas or seedless raisins

Sieve together the flour, salt and spices. Cream the butter and sugar together until light and fluffy. Beat in the egg and treacle and one-quarter of the flour mixture. Mix the bicarbonate of soda and milk and stir a little into the cake mixture. Add the fruit, remaining flour mixture and remaining liquid. Mix well and turn into a greased rectangular tin 11 × 7 in (27·5 × 17·5 cm). Bake at 350°F/180°C/Gas Mark 4 for 45 minutes. Turn out and cool on a wire rack. Wrap in foil or polythene to freeze.

To serve
Thaw at room temperature for 3 hours and cut in squares.
High Quality Storage Life   4 months

Orange Frost Cake

4 oz/100 g butter
2 oz/50 g caster sugar
2 tablespoons/30 ml clear honey
grated rind of ½ orange
2 eggs
5 oz/125 g self-raising flour
2 tablespoons/30 ml orange juice
Icing
4 oz/100 g butter
6 oz/150 g icing sugar
1 tablespoon/15 ml clear honey
1 tablespoon/15 ml hot water

Cream the butter and sugar together until light and fluffy. Beat in the honey and orange rind and add eggs gradually. Fold in the flour and then add the orange juice and mix to a soft dropping consistency. Put into a greased and lined 8 in/20 cm round sandwich tin. Bake at 375°F/190°C/Gas Mark 5 for 25 minutes. Turn out and cool on a wire rack. To make the icing: soften the butter and beat in the sifted icing sugar. Beat in the honey and water, and a few drops of orange colouring if liked. Beat until creamy and smooth and spread on the cake, making soft peaks with the back of a teaspoon. Open-freeze and then wrap in foil or polythene for freezer storage.

To serve
Thaw at room temperature for 3 hours. Decorate with mimosa balls or crystallised orange slices if liked.
High Quality Storage Life   4 months

Ice cake is made with a sponge base and three varieties of bought ice-cream. It can be served as an unusual birthday cake.

Walnut Brownies

6 oz/150 g margarine
1 oz/25 g cocoa
6 oz/150 g caster sugar
2 eggs
2 oz/50 g plain flour
2 oz/50 g chopped walnuts

Melt 2 oz/50 g margarine and stir in the cocoa. Set aside to cool. Cream the remaining margarine with the sugar until soft and gradually beat in the eggs. Fold in the sieved flour and add the chopped walnuts and cocoa mixture. Put into a greased and base-lined 7 in/17·5 cm tin and bake at 350°F/180°C/ Gas Mark 4 for 45 minutes. Cool and turn out. Wrap in foil or polythene to freeze.
To serve
Thaw at room temperature for 3 hours and sprinkle with caster sugar, or cover with melted plain chocolate. Cut in squares to serve as a cake, or as a pudding with whipped cream or ice cream.
High Quality Storage Life   4 months

Ice Cream Layer Cake

1 round sponge cake
chocolate ice cream
strawberry ice cream
vanilla ice cream
sweetened whipped cream

Use a bought or home-made sponge cake for the base of this cake and place in a deep spring-form tin. Use soft ice cream to make the other layers. Put scoops of chocolate ice cream on the sponge cake base and smooth with a palette knife. Top with a layer of strawberry ice cream and then a layer of vanilla ice cream (or use any other favourite combination of flavours). Cover with foil and put in the freezer until firm. Remove the spring-form sides of the tin and decorate the cake with swirls of sweetened whipped cream. Open freeze until the cream is firm and then put into a rigid container for storage. If you do not wish to have the base of your cake tin left in the freezer, use the spring-form sides of the tin on a cake board base, ready for serving.
To serve

Apricot pastries made with puff pastry are a delicious treat at coffee- or tea-time.

Put on to a serving plate and decorate with chocolate curls or fresh fruit. Cut in slices like a cake.
High Quality Storage Life   1 month

Apricot Pastries

12 oz/350 g puff pastry
12 canned apricot halves
beaten egg to glaze
3 oz/75 g apricot jam

Roll out the pastry into a large square. Divide into 14 squares. Put 12 pastry squares on to a baking sheet and place an apricot half in the centre of each. Cut the remaining squares into 24 strips and cross two strips over each apricot half. Brush pastry with the beaten egg and bake at 425°F/220°C/Gas Mark 7 for 20 minutes until the pastry is risen and crisp. Lift on to a wire rack and brush with hot melted jam. Cool and pack in a rigid container to freeze.
To serve
Thaw at room temperature for 1 hour, or reheat at 350°F/180°C/Gas Mark 4 for 15 minutes.
High Quality Storage Life   2 months

Basic Scones

1 lb/450 g plain white flour
1 teaspoon bicarbonate of soda
2 teaspoons cream of tartar
3 oz/75 g butter
$\frac{1}{4}$ pint/125 ml milk

Sift together the flour, soda and cream of tartar and rub in butter until the mixture is like breadcrumbs. Mix with the milk to make a soft dough. Roll out and cut into circles, and place close together on a greased baking sheet. Bake at 450°F/230°C/Gas Mark 8 for 12 minutes and cool. Pack in polythene bags to freeze.
Fruit Scones   Add 1$\frac{1}{2}$ oz/40 g sugar and 2 oz/50 g dried fruit.
Cheese Scones   Add a pinch each of salt and pepper and 3 oz/75 g grated cheese.
To serve
Thaw in wrappings at room temperature for 1 hour, or heat at 350°F/180°C/Gas Mark 4 for 10 minutes with a covering of foil.
High Quality Storage Life   4 months

Danish pastry pinwheels are made from a yeast pastry and they may be frozen plain or with icing.

Danish Pastry Pinwheels

8 oz/225 g strong white (bread) flour
½ teaspoon salt
2½ oz/65 g sugar
½ oz/15 g fresh yeast
¼ pint/125 ml warm butter
3 oz/75 g butter
3 oz/75 g mixed dried fruit
beaten egg to glaze
water icing

Put flour and salt into a warm basin. Cream the yeast with a little of the sugar and put into the flour with the remaining sugar and water. Mix to a soft, slightly sticky dough, and leave to rise in a warm place until increased by one-third in volume. Form butter into a rectangle and dust with flour. Flatten the dough with the hands and fold with the fat in the centre like a parcel. Roll and fold twice like puff pastry. Leave in a cold place for 20 minutes, then roll and fold twice more and leave for 20 minutes. Roll out to ½ in/1·25 cm thickness and sprinkle with dried fruit. Roll up like a Swiss roll and cut into ½ in/ 1·25 cm slices. Place on baking sheet and brush with beaten egg. Bake at 375°F/190°C/Gas Mark 5 for 30 minutes. Cool on a wire rack. The pastries may be frozen un-iced or with a light water icing. Pack in foil trays with a foil lid or put the trays into poly-thene bags.

To serve

Remove wrappings and thaw at room temperature for 1 hour.

High Quality Storage Life   2 months

Currant buns freeze well and make a good snack with a glass of milk.

Drop Scones

8 oz/225 g plain flour
$\frac{1}{4}$ teaspoon salt
$\frac{1}{2}$ teaspoon bicarbonate of soda
1 teaspoon cream of tartar
1 oz/25 g sugar
1 egg
$\frac{1}{2}$ pint/250 ml milk

Sieve together the flour, salt, soda and cream of tartar. Stir in sugar and mix to a batter with egg and milk. Cook in spoonfuls on a lightly greased griddle or frying pan. When bubbles appear on the surface turn and cook other side. Cool in a cloth to keep soft. Pack in a rigid container with Clingfilm between the layers to freeze.
To serve
Thaw at room temperature for 1 hour and spread with butter.
High Quality Storage Life   2 months

Currant Buns

For the Batter
4 oz/100 g strong plain (bread) flour
1 teaspoon sugar
1 oz/25 g fresh yeast
$\frac{1}{4}$ pint/125 ml warm milk
$\frac{1}{4}$ pint/125 ml warm water less 4 tablespoons/ 60 ml
For the Dough
12 oz/350 g strong plain flour
1 teaspoon salt
2 oz/50 g sugar
2 oz/50 g butter or margarine
1 egg
4 oz/100 g currants
To Glaze
2 oz/50 g sugar
4 tablespoons/60 ml water

Blend the batter ingredients together in a large bowl and set aside for 20–30 minutes until the batter froths. Mix the dough ingredients, rubbing the fat into the flour with the sugar and salt, and mixing with the beaten egg and currants, and work in the frothy batter. Mix to a dough which is soft and leaves the sides of the bowl clean. Knead for about 5 minutes on a lightly floured board until smooth and not sticky. Put the dough into a lightly greased polythene bag, loosely tied and leave for about 1$\frac{1}{2}$ hours at room temperature until doubled in size.

Turn the dough on to a floured surface and flatten with the knuckles to knock out air bubbles. Knead to a firm dough and divide into 14 pieces. Shape into balls, working the dough until it is smooth. Put the buns well apart on a lightly floured baking sheet and flatten them slightly with the palm of the hand. Put inside a lightly greased polythene bag and leave to rise about 30 minutes until the dough is springy. Take off the bag, and bake at buns at 425°F/220°C/ Gas Mark 7 for 15–20 minutes until golden brown. Just before taking the buns from the oven, dissolve the sugar and water for the glaze. As soon as the buns are ready, put them on to a wire rack and brush liberally with the glaze. Leave until cool, pack into a polythene bag and freeze.
To serve
Thaw at room temperature for 1 hour, or reheat at 350°F/180°C/Gas Mark 4 for 10 minutes.
High Quality Storage Life   4 months

Brioches

8 oz/225 g strong white (bread) flour
1 oz/25 g yeast
2 tablespoons/30 ml warm water
3 eggs
6 oz/150 g melted butter
1 teaspoon salt
½ oz/15 g sugar

Put 2 oz/50 g flour into a warm bowl and mix with yeast creamed with warm water. Put the little ball of dough into a bowl of warm water and it will expand and form a sponge. Put the remaining flour into a bowl and beat in the eggs thoroughly. Add the butter, salt and sugar and continue beating. Add the yeast sponge drained from the water and mix well. Cover the bowl with a damp cloth and leave in a warm place for 2 hours to rise. Knead the dough

Brioche is a fine, sweet bread which may be eaten plain, with jam, or given a sweet or savoury filling.

well, cover the bowl and leave in a cool place overnight. Half-fill castle pudding tins or fluted moulds with dough and top with smaller balls of dough. Leave in a warm place for 30 minutes. Brush with a little milk and bake at 450°F/230°C/Gas Mark 8 for 15 minutes. Cool and pack in bags to freeze.

To serve
Thaw at room temperature for 45 minutes to serve with butter. Brioches may be heated, the tops removed and the centre lightly scooped out and filled with a sweet or savoury mixture (fruit in syrup; creamed chicken; shrimps) and the tops replaced for service.

High Quality Storage Life   2 months

Ring doughnuts are made with yeast and deep-fried. It is best to toss them in sugar when they have thawed.

Ring Doughnuts

8 oz/225 g strong white (bread) flour
1 teaspoon salt
2 teaspoons sugar
½ oz/15 g fresh yeast
¾ pint/375 ml lukewarm milk
½ oz/15 g margarine

Sieve the flour and salt and mix in the sugar. Whisk the yeast in half the milk. Add margarine to remaining milk and cool to lukewarm. Mix both liquids into the flour and knead well. Cover and leave in a warm place for 1 hour. Knead lightly and then roll out to 1 in/2·5 cm thick. Cut out 3 in/7·5 cm circles and then cut out centres with 1 in/2·5 cm cutter. Roll out the cut-out centres and cut into extra rings as before. Put on baking trays and leave in a warm place for 20 minutes to rise. Fry two or three at a time in hot oil until golden-brown and drain very well on kitchen paper. Cool and pack in polythene bags to freeze.

To serve
Heat straight from the freezer at 400°F/200°C/Gas Mark 6 for 8 minutes. Roll in caster sugar and serve at once.
High Quality Storage Life   1 month

178

Marmalade cake is easy to bake and has a fine flavour of orange marmalade which is very appetising.

Marmalade Cake

6 oz/150 g butter
6 oz/150 g caster sugar
3 eggs
10 oz/300 g self-raising flour
3 tablespoons chunky marmalade
2 oz/50 g chopped mixed peel
grated peel of 1 orange
5 tablespoons/75 ml water

Beat the butter and sugar together until light and creamy. Beat in the egg yolks, one at a time, then one tablespoon of the flour. Stir in the marmalade, peel, orange rind and water, and fold in the remaining flour. Whisk the egg whites to soft peaks and fold into the cake mixture. Turn into a greased and lined 7 in/17·5 cm cake tin and bake at 350°F/180°C/Gas Mark 4 for 1¼ hours. Cool on a wire rack and wrap in polythene to freeze.
To serve
Thaw at room temperature for 3 hours.
High Quality Storage Life   4 months

Crumble Cake

8 oz/225 g plain flour
4 oz/100 g sugar
6 oz/150 g margarine
2 teaspoons grated orange or lemon peel

Stir the sugar into the flour and rub in the fat until the mixture looks like fine breadcrumbs. Add the grated rind. Spread in a greased shallow tin and press down lightly. Bake at 325°F/170°C/Gas Mark 3 for 30 minutes. Cool in the tin and cut in slices. Pack in a rigid container to freeze.
To serve
Thaw at room temperature for 3 hours. This cake is very good to serve with fruit or ice cream.
High Quality Storage Life   4 months

Gingerbread loaf is very good sliced, spread with butter, or it can make a delicious pudding served with fruit and cream.

Gingerbread Loaf

4 oz/100 g self-raising flour
$\frac{1}{4}$ teaspoon salt
1 teaspoon ground ginger
2 oz/50 g soft brown sugar
1 oz/25 g fine oatmeal
3 oz/75 g lard
3 oz/75 g golden syrup
1 teaspoon/5 ml warm milk
1 egg

Sieve the flour, salt and ginger into a bowl. Stir in the sugar and oatmeal. Put the lard and syrup into a saucepan and heat until the lard has melted. Add the milk. Mix into the dry ingredients and beat in the egg. Beat well and pour into a 7 in/17·5 cm greased loaf tin. Bake at 325°F/170°C/Gas Mark 3 for 1$\frac{1}{4}$ hours. Cool on a wire rack and pack in polythene to freeze.

To serve
Unwrap and thaw at room temperature for 3 hours. Serve in slices, with butter if liked.

High Quality Storage Life　4 months

Chocolate cake may be iced or simply dusted with icing sugar and may be eaten as a cake or as a pudding.

One-Step Chocolate Cake

1 tablespoon cocoa
2 tablespoons/30 ml milk
4 oz/100 g soft margarine
5 oz/125 g caster sugar
2 eggs
4 oz/100 g self-raising flour

Put all the ingredients into a bowl and blend with a wooden spoon or mixer until light and fluffy. Put into a greased 8 in/20 cm round tin and bake at 350°F/180°C/Gas Mark 4 for 40 minutes. Cool on a wire rack. Pack in polythene to freeze.
To serve
Unwrap and thaw at room temperature for 3 hours. Sprinkle with icing sugar or cover with chocolate icing. Serve as a cake, or as a pudding with whipped cream.
High Quality Storage Life   4 months

Chocolate Truffle Cake

4 oz/100 g margarine
1 oz/25 g sugar
1 tablespoon golden syrup
1 oz/25 g cocoa
8 oz/225 g sweet biscuit crumbs
2 oz/50 g plain chocolate

Cream the margarine and sugar and add the syrup and cocoa. Crush the biscuits very finely with a rolling pin. Add gradually to the mixture and stir well. Press down into a greased tin so that the mixture is about $\frac{1}{2}$ in/1·25 cm thick. Melt the chocolate in a bowl over hot water and pour over the cake. Leave in a cool place to set and mark into squares. Leave in the tin and wrap in foil or polythene to freeze. The cake may be made in a foil tray if preferred.
To serve
Thaw at room temperature for 3 hours and cut in squares. This is a delicious cake and can also be used as a base for ice cream – it is particularly good with a topping of coffee ice cream.

Chocolate Roll

4 oz/100 g self-raising flour
pinch of salt
3 oz/75 g butter or margarine
3 oz/75 g caster sugar
2 eggs
2 drops vanilla essence

For the icing
5 oz/125 g butter
8 oz/225 g icing sugar
8 oz/225 g plain chocolate
1 tablespoon/15 ml rum
2 oz/50 g chopped nuts

Sieve the flour and salt. Cream the butter or margarine and sugar until light and fluffy. Beat in the eggs one at a time with a little of the flour mixture, then stir in the remaining flour and essence. Spread evenly in a lined Swiss roll tin and bake at 425°F/220°C/Gas Mark 7 for 10 minutes. Turn out on to a piece of sugared greaseproof paper. Trim off edges and roll quickly with paper inside. Make the icing by creaming the butter and icing sugar. Melt the chocolate in a bowl over hot water and work it into the butter mixture with the rum. When the cake is cold, unroll carefully and spread half the icing on the surface. Roll up tightly and cover the cake with the remaining icing. Sprinkle with chopped nuts. Green pistachio nuts look particularly attractive. Open-freeze and then pack in polythene or a rigid container for storage.
To serve
Remove wrappings and thaw at room temperature for 3 hours. Serve as a cake in thin slices, or use for a pudding with rum-flavoured sweetened whipped cream.
High Quality Storage Life 2 months

Chocolate roll: a rich chocolate gâteau which is suitable for tea-time or for a party pudding.

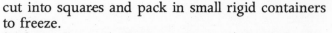

Freezer Fudge

1 lb/450 g granulated sugar
2 oz/50 g butter
$\frac{1}{4}$ pint/125 ml evaporated milk
$\frac{1}{4}$ pint/125 ml water
$\frac{1}{2}$ teaspoon vanilla essence

Put the sugar, butter, evaporated milk and water into a thick saucepan and heat gently until the butter has melted and the sugar has dissolved. Bring to the boil and heat to 237°F/114°C*, stirring occasionally Take off the heat, add the essence and beat until smooth and creamy. If liked, add some finely chopped nuts. Pour into a greased shallow tin and mark into squares when nearly set. When set, cut into squares and pack in small rigid containers to freeze.

* If you have no thermometer, test the fudge by dropping a little into a cup of cold water when it looks thick and creamy in the saucepan. If the drops in the water can be rolled together in the fingers to form a soft ball, the fudge has reached the correct temperature for beating.
To serve
Thaw for 2 hours at room temperature.
High Quality Storage Life 4 months

Freezer fudge is easily made in a variety of flavours and keeps beautifully fresh in the freezer.

Sugar biscuits are easily made and their flavour may be varied by the addition of nuts and fruit peels to the recipe.

Sugar Biscuits

4 oz/100 g butter
8 oz/225 g caster sugar
1 egg
1 tablespoon/15 ml milk
$\frac{1}{2}$ teaspoon vanilla essence
6 oz/150 g plain flour
$\frac{1}{2}$ teaspoon baking powder
$\frac{1}{2}$ teaspoon salt

Soften the butter and work in the sugar, egg, milk and vanilla. Add the sifted flour, baking powder and salt and work into a firm dough. Roll out thinly and cut with a fluted cutter. Put on to greased baking sheets and bake at 375°F/190°C/Gas Mark 5 for 10 minutes. Lift on to a wire rack, sprinkle with a little granulated or Demerara sugar and cool. To freeze, pack into rigid containers.
To serve
Thaw at room temperature for 20 minutes.
High Quality Storage Life 2 months

Variations

1) Use brown sugar instead of caster sugar; add 1 oz/25 g chopped nuts if liked.
2) Add 1 oz/25 g cocoa to basic biscuits; *or* flavour with 1 teaspoon ground ginger; *or* with $\frac{1}{2}$ teaspoon lemon essence instead of vanilla.

Marshmallow Biscuits

$1\frac{1}{2}$ oz/40 g butter
8 oz/225 g marshmallows
4 oz/100 g plain chocolate
4 oz/100 g Rice Krispies cereal

Put the butter into a bowl over hot water, or into the top of a double saucepan. Melt and stir in the marshmallows and broken chocolate. Stir until smooth and creamy. Put the cereal into a bowl and stir in the chocolate mixture. Put into a greased tin about 1 in/2·5 cm thick. Leave for about 1 hour until cold and firm. Cut into squares and pack in a rigid container to freeze.

Marsmallow biscuits are a great favourite with children and they can help to make them.

Nut slices are made from shortbread with a creamy walnut filling and may be iced or dusted with sugar.

To serve
Thaw at room temperature for 2 hours.
High Quality Storage Life　4 months

Nut Slices

12 oz/350 g plain flour
4 oz/100 g caster sugar
8 oz/225 g butter

Filling
5 oz/125 g caster sugar
$\frac{1}{4}$ pint/125 ml single cream
5 oz/125 g walnuts
1 tablespoon/15 ml rum

Sieve flour into a basin and stir in the sugar. Work in the butter until the mixture looks like breadcrumbs. Knead well and divide the dough into two pieces. Roll out one piece carefully to line a square or rectangular tin. Make the filling by heating the sugar until it melts and stirring in the cream,

ground walnuts and rum. Leave to cool and then spread on to the pastry base. Roll out the remaining pastry and cover the filling. Bake at 350°F/180°C/ Gas Mark 4 for 40 minutes. Cool and cut into pieces. Pack in a rigid container to freeze.
To serve
Thaw at room temperature for 3 hours. If liked, dust with caster sugar or icing sugar, or top with a little water icing.
High Quality Storage Life　2 months

Sponge Cake

3 eggs
3 oz/75 g caster sugar
3 oz/75 g plain flour
½ teaspoon baking powder

Warm bowl and whisk slightly. Put eggs and sugar in bowl and mix until eggs are thick, white and fluffy. Fold in sifted flour and baking powder. Put into greased 6 in/15 cm cake tin, and bake at 350°F/180°C/Gas Mark 4 for 50 minutes. The cake may also be baked in two 8 in/20 cm sandwich tins at 400°F/200°C/Gas Mark 6 for 15 minutes. When done, turn the cake on to a wire rack. Wrap in foil or polythene.
To serve
Thaw at room temperature for 3 hours.
High Quality Storage Life   2 months

Madeira Cake

9 oz/250 g plain flour
1 teaspoon baking powder
pinch of salt
6 oz/150 g caster sugar
6 oz/150 g butter
3 eggs
1 teaspoon grated lemon rind
1 teaspoon grated orange rind
milk or rum to mix

Sift the flour with the baking powder and salt. Warm a mixing bowl and beater. Put the sugar and butter in the bowl and beat until white and fluffy. Add the eggs one at a time, beating well each time. Fold in the flour and orange and lemon rind. Add a little milk, or, for a richer cake, rum, if necessary. The mixture should shake easily from a spoon. Put in a lined 7 in/17·5 cm cake tin and bake at 350°F/170°C/Gas Mark 4 for 1 hour and 20 minutes. Cool on a wire rack and wrap in foil to freeze.
To serve
Thaw at room temperature for 3 hours.
High Quality Storage Life   2 months

Picnic Tea Loaf

1 lb/450 g mixed dried fruit
8 oz/225 g sugar
½ pint/250 ml warm tea
1 egg
2 tablespoons marmalade
1 lb/450 g self-raising flour

Soak fruit with sugar and tea overnight. Stir egg and marmalade into fruit and mix well with flour. Pour into two 1 lb loaf tins and bake at 325°F/170°C/Gas Mark 3 for 1¾ hours. Cool in tins for 15 minutes before turning out. Cool. Pack in polythene bags or foil.
To serve
Thaw for 3 hours, slice and butter.
High Quality Storage Life   4 months

Sponge cakes can be bulk-baked, and are always a useful sweet item for the freezer.

Madeira cake

Éclairs are easily made from choux pastry and may be covered with either chocolate or coffee icing.

Fruit and Nut Shortcake

4 tablespoons/60 ml orange juice
4 oz/100 g seedless raisins
4 oz/100 g nut kernels
6 oz/150 g plain flour
2 oz/50 g caster sugar
4 oz/100 g butter

Put the orange juice and raisins into a saucepan and bring slowly to the boil. Remove from the heat, mash lightly with a fork and stir in the coarsely chopped nuts. Sieve the flour into a basin and stir in the sugar. Work in the butter until the mixture looks like breadcrumbs. Knead well and divide the dough into two pieces. Roll out into two rounds, one slightly larger than the other. Use the larger round to line a 7 in/17·5 cm sandwich tin. Fill with the nut and raisin mixture and top with the second round of pastry. Seal the edges with a little water and mark with a fork. Prick all over with a fork. Bake at 350°F/180°C/Gas Mark 4 for 45 minutes. Cool in the tin. Pack in polythene to freeze.
To serve
Thaw at room temperature for 3 hours and dust with sugar. Serve on its own or with sweetened whipped cream.
High Quality Storage Life   4 months

Éclairs

¼ pint/125 ml water
2 oz/50 g lard
2¼ oz/58 g plain flour
pinch of salt
2 small eggs

Put the water and lard into a pan and bring to the boil. Tip in the flour and salt and draw the pan from the heat. Beat until smooth with a wooden spoon. Cook for 3 minutes, beating very thoroughly so that the mixture is smooth and is not sticking to the sides of the pan. Cool. Whisk the eggs together and add small quantities of the egg to the flour mixture. Beat well between each addition until the mixture is soft and firm but holds its shape – it may not be necessary to add all the egg. Pipe in finger-lengths on to baking sheets and bake at 425°F/220°C/Gas Mark 7 for 30 minutes. Cool on a rack, making a small slit in each to allow any steam to escape. Pack in polythene bags to freeze.
To serve
Thaw in wrappings at room temperature for 1 hour. Take off wrappings and put éclairs on to a baking sheet. Heat at 350°F/180°F/Gas Mark 4 for 5 minutes. Cool and fill with lightly sweetened whipped cream. Top with chocolate or coffee glacé icing.
High Quality Storage Life   4 months

Index

Acid pack 60
Air exclusion 15
Appetisers 84
Apple Dumplings, Baked 164
Apples 40, 88
Apple Sauce 154
Apple Tart, Sliced 169
Apricot Tart, Sliced 169
Apricot Crumble, Crunchy 165
Apricot Pastries 173
Apricots 40
Artichokes, globe 27
    Jerusalem 27
Asparagus 27
Asparagus Flan 138
Aubergines 28
Avocado Pears 40, 88

Babas 75
Bacon 53
Bacon Pasties 136
Baked Apple Dumplings 164
Baked Leeks 146
Banana Bread 171
Bananas 40, 88
Basic Chicken Stock 95
Basic Poultry Stuffing 154
Basic Scones 173
Bean Casserole 142
Beans, broad 28
    French 28
    in Tomato Sauce 148
    runner 28
Beef 47
Beef Casserole, Spiced 120
Beef in Beer 120
Beetroot 28
Beetroot Soup 99
Berkshire Pigs 158
Biscuits 69, 75
Blackberries 40
Blackcurrant Pie 161
Blackcurrants 41
Blanching 26
Bloaters 64
Blueberries 40
Bombes 67
Bread 20, 69, 75
Bread dough 75
Bread, fruit and nut 75
Bread Pudding 162
Bread Rolls 78

Bread, sliced 75
Breast of Lamb Casserole 125
Breast of Veal with Sausage Stuffing 126
Brine pack 60
Brioche 75, 176
Broccoli 28
Brown Veal Casserole 127
Brussels sprouts 28
Bulk buying 19
Bulk cooking 24
Buns 78
Butter 65
Butters, flavoured 85

Cabbage, green 28, 88
    red 28
Cakes 20, 69
    butter-iced 75
Canapés 84
Carrots 28
Carrot Soup 95
Casseroles 50, 81
Cassoulet 127
Cauliflower 29
Celery 29, 88
Celery Soup 91
Cheese 65
Cheesecake, Lemon 164
Cheesecake with Raspberries 164
Cheese Loaf 133
Cherries 41
Cherry Crumble 161
Cherry Stuffing 157
Chestnut Stuffing 157
Chestnuts 29
Chicken 56
Chicken in Tomato Sauce 113
Chicken Liver Pâté 100
Chicken Patties 114
Chicken Pie, Country 114
Chicken Soup, Spring 95
Chicory 29, 88
Chicory with Cheese 136
Chives 30
Chocolate Cake, One-Step 181
Chocolate Ice Cream 161
Chocolate Roll 182
Chocolate Truffle Cake 181
Chops 52
Choux pastry 77
Chunkey Pâté 101
Cock-a-Leekie Soup 95

Coconut 41
Cod 64
Cod with Curry Sauce 108
Cod's Roe Pâté 100
Coffee Fruit Buns 170
Cooked Fish 82
Cooked Meat 80
Cooked Poultry 81
Cooking in bulk 24
Coq Au Vin 113
Cornish Fish Pasties 136
Corn-on-the-cob 29
Country Chicken Pie 114
Crab 61
Cranberries 41
Cranberry Sauce 156
Crayfish 62
Cream 66
    soured 87
Cream buns 77
Cream cheese 66
Cream ice 68
Croissants 77
Croûtons 80
Crumble Cake 179
Crumpets 77
Crunchy Apricot Crumble 165
Cubed meat 50
Cucumber 30
Cumberland Cutlets 129
Currant Buns 175
Currants, black, red and white 41
Custard 87
Custard Ice 68

Dairy produce 65
Damsons 42
Danish pastries 77
Danish Pastry Pinwheels 174
Dates 42
Dehydration 16
Dips 84
Discolouration of fruit 36
Doughnuts 77, 178
Drop Scones 77, 175
Dry pack 60
Dry sugar pack 36
Duck 56
Duck with Orange 117

Éclairs 77, 189
Eel 64

Egg whites 66
Egg yolks 66
Eggs 66
   hard-boiled 87
Electrical power failure 13
Equipment 24

Family Fruit Cake 170
Farmhouse Chicken 115
Fennel 30
Figs 42
Fish 60
Fish Cakes 103
Fish Puffs 107
Fish Rarebit 104
Fish Pasties, Cornish, 136
Fish Pie 137
Fish Pudding 133
Flan cases 72
Flans (see also Quiches) 72, 83
Flavourings and decorations, cake 70
Foods to avoid freezing 87
Freezer burns 16
Freezer Fudge 182
Freezers, chest 12
   choice of 11
   cleaning 13
   defrosting 13
   installation 13
   upright 12
Freezing,
   fast- 13
   foods to avoid 87
   temperatures 6
Fruit and Nut Shortcake 189
Fruit, fillings for pies 71
   freezing
   juices 37
   purées 37
   syrups 37
Fruit Cake, Family, Light 76
Fruit Flan Pastry 158

Galantines 81
Game 56
Garlic 87
Gelatine ice 68
Giblets 56
Gingerbread Loaf 180
Ginger Fruit Cake 171
Glazing fish 60
Goose 57
Gooseberries 42
Gooseberry Sauce 154
Goulash 118
Grapefruit 42
Grapes 42
Gravy 88
Greengages 42
Green Pea Soup 91
Green peppers 32
Grouse 57
Guavas 43
Guinea fowl 57

Haddock 62, 64
Halibut 62
Halibut in tomato sauce 107
Ham 51
Hare 58

Hare Soup 98
Headspace 15, 36
Herb cubes 80
Herbs 30, 87
Hermits 170
High quality storage life, bakery goods 87
   cooked dishes 87
   dairy produce 87
   fish 86
   fruit 86
   game 86
   meat 86
   poultry 86
   vegetables 86
Hot Kipper Pastries 107
Hot Tartare Sauce 157
Hot water crust pies 71

Ice cream 21, 66–7
Ice cream flavourings 68
Ice Cream Layer Cake 172
Ice Cream Sundaes 166
Ice crystals 16
Icings 70
Insurance 11
Italian Tomato Soup 91

Jam fruit 37
Joints 51

Kale 30
Kedgeree 104
Kidneys 51
Kidneys in Red Wine 129
Kidney Soup 92
Kipper and Cheese Pizza 103
Kipper Mousse 100
Kippers 64
Kohlrabi 30
Kumquats 43

Labelling 18
Lamb 48
Lamb and Lentil Bake 120
Lamb Pie, Savoury 132
Lamb Stew, Winter 125
Leeks 31
Leek Soup 93
Lemon Cheesecake 164
Lemons 43
Limes 43
Lincolnshire Haslet 130
Liquid capacity 11
Little Meat Balls 118
Liver 51
Liver and Sausage Bake 102
Liver Pâté 101
Liver Loaf 130
Lobster 62
Loganberries 43

Macaroni Cheese 134
Mackerel 62, 64
Madeira Cake 186
Maître d'Hôtel Butter 155
Mangoes 44
Margarine 65
Marmalade Cake 179
Marrow 31
Marshmallow Biscuits 184

Mayonnaise 87
Measures and weights 6
Meat, choosing for the freezer 47
Meat Balls, Little 118
Meat fillings for pies 71
Meat loaves 81
Meat puddings 52
Melon 44, 88
Milk 66, 88
Minced meat 52
Mint 30
Mixed Vegetable Casserole 143
Moulds 67
Mousses 84
Muffins 78
Mushroom Pizza, Quick 130
Mushrooms 31
Mushroom Vol-Au-Vent 137
Mussels 62
Mutton 48

Nectarines 44
Noodles 83
Normandy Rabbit 133
Nut Ice Cream 168
Nut Slices 185

Offal 51
One-Step Chocolate Cake 181
Onions 32, 87
Onion Soup 99
Open freezing baked goods 74
Open tarts 72
Orange Frost Cake 171
Orange Stuffing 157
Oranges 44
Oven temperatures, domestic 6
Oxidation 16
Oxtail Soup 96
Oysters 62

Packaging 15
Packaging materials 14
Pancakes 78
   savoury 139
   sweet 163
Parsley 30
Parsnips 32
Partridge 57
Pasta 82, 83
Pastries, Danish 174
Pastry 70, 78
Pastry cases 78
   baked and unbaked 70
Pâtés 81, 100
Peaches 44
Pears 44, 88
Peas, edible pod 32
   green 32
Pea Soup, Green 91
Peppers, green and red 32
Persimmons 45
Pheasant 57
Picnic Tea Loaf 186
Pies, baked 71
   meat 51
   unbaked 71
Pigeon 58
Pineapple 45
Piquant Pastry Sauce 156

Pizza 72
Plaice 64
Plover 58
Plums 45
Pomegranates 45
Pork 48
Pork Carbonnade 118
Pork Casserole 124
Potato Croquettes 149
Potatoes 33, 87
Potted Crab 106
Poultry 55
Poultry Stuffing, Basic 154
Power failure 13
Prawn Pizza 112
Prawn Quiche 112
Prawns 63
Pudding sauces 84
Puddings, baked 84
    freezing 83
    fruit 84
    gelatine 84
    steamed 84
Pumpkin 33
Purées, fruit 37

Quail 58
Quiche Lorraine 134
Quiches 72
Quick Mushroom Pizza 130
Quinces 45

Rabbit 58
Rancidity 16
Raspberries 45
Raspberry Tart 160
Ratatouille 141
Recording 18
Redcurrants 41
Red peppers 32
Rhubarb 46
Rice 83, 87
Rich Fruit Cake 77
Ring Doughnuts 178
Rolls 78
Royal icing 87
Rump steak 47
Running costs 11

Salmon 62, 64
Salmon and Smoked Haddock
    Turnovers 107

Sandwiches 72, 78–9
Sardine Pâté 100
Sauces 83, 88
Sausage meat 52
Sausage Stuffing 156
Sausages 52
Savarins 75
Savoury flans (see Quiches) 72, 83
Savoury Lamb Pie 132
Savoury Pancakes 139
Scallops 63
Scallops with Mushrooms 109
Scones, basic 79
    drop 77, 175
Sea Pie 106
Seafood Flan 103
Shellfish 61
Shepherd's Pie 52
Shrimps 64
Simple Pork Pâté 102
Sirloin 47
Slab cakes 77
Sliced Apple Tart 169
Smoked fish 61
Smoked Haddock Cobbler 104
Snacks 84
Snipe 58
Sole 64
Solid ice pack 60
Sorbets 168
Soufflés 84
Soup garnishes 80
Soups 80
Spaghetti 87
Spaghetti Bolognese 132
Spiced Beef Casserole 120
Spices 87
Spinach 33
Spinach Flan 153
Spinach Noodles with Cheese 135
Sponge cake 76, 186
Sprats 64
Spring Chicken Soup 95
Star system 10
Steak 52
Steak and Kidney Pie 121
Stews 50, 81
Storage, bulk 19
    long-term 10
    short-term 10
Strawberries 46
Stuffed Artichokes 147

Stuffed Aubergines 143
Stuffed Cabbage Rolls 121
Stuffed Courgettes in Tomato Sauce 141
Stuffed Onions 146
Stuffed Peppers 152
Stuffings 58
Sugar Biscuits 184
Sweet and Sour Cabbage 149
Sweet and Sour Lamb 125
Syrup pack 36

Tangerine Ice 168
Temperatures, deep-fat frying 6
    oven 6
    star system 10
    sugar-boiling 6
Tomatoes 33, 88
Tomato Sauce 154
Tomato Soup, Italian 91
Tongue 51
Tripe 52
Trout 62, 64
Turbot 62
Turkey 59
Turkey Soup 96
Turnips 34

Unsweetened dry pack 36
Unsweetened wet pack 36

Veal with Olives 125
Vegetable purée 34
Vegetables, cooking 27
    freezing 26
    in sauce 34
Venison 59

Waffles 79, 166
Walnut Brownies 172
Weights and measures 6
Welsh Teacakes 170
Whipped cream 66
White currants 41
White fish 64
Whitebait 107
Whiting 64
Winter Lamb Stew 125
Woodcock 58
Wrapping materials 16–17

Yeast 79
Yeast mixtures, uncooked 69